CONTENTS

BORDERS &

BOUNDARIES

LEFT BANK

Number 5

Blue Heron Publishing, Inc.
Hillsboro, Oregon

Editor: Linny Stovall

Associate Editor: Stephen J. Beard

Publisher: Dennis Stovall

Staff: Erin Leonard, Frank Marquardt

Copyeditor: Mary Catherine Lamb

Advertising: Linny Stovall

Interior Design: Dennis Stovall

Cover Art: Virginia Flynn

Cover Design: Marcia Barrentine

Advisors: Ann Chandonnet, Madeline DeFrees, David James Duncan, Katherine Dunn, Jim Hepworth, Ursula K. Le Guin, Lynda Sexson, J. T. Stewart, Alan Twigg, Lyle Weis, Shawn Wong.

Editorial correspondence: Linny Stovall or Stephen Beard, *Left Bank*, Blue Heron Publishing, Inc., 24450 N.W. Hansen Road, Hillsboro, Oregon 97124. Submissions are welcome if accompanied by a stamped, self-addressed envelope. Otherwise they will not be returned. Authors must have a strong connection to the Pacific Northwest. Submissions are read during a period beginning one month before the deadline (see current guidelines) and ending one month after. Editorial guidelines are available on request (include SASE).

Left Bank is a series of thematic collections published semiannually by Blue Heron Publishing, Inc., 24450 N.W. Hansen Road, Hillsboro, Oregon 97124. Single editions are $9.95US (plus $2 s&h). Subscriptions (two editions) are available for $16. *Left Bank* is distributed to the book trade and libraries in the United States by Consortium Book Sales and Distribution, 1045 Westgate Drive, Saint Paul, Minnesota 55114-1065; and in Canada by Orca Book Publishers, Ltd., Box 5626, Station B, Victoria, B.C. V8V 3W1.

"Refugee Camp" is excerpted with permission from *Rooms in the House of Stone* by Michael Dorris, Milkweed Editions. An earlier version of "Nothing North of Disneyland" appeared in *Dandelion*. A version of "The Real Northwest Economy" appeared, in a slightly different form, in the Winter 1992 issue of *Old Oregon*, the University of Oregon alumni magazine.

Publication of this edition is made possible in part by a grant from the Oregon Institute of Literary Arts.

Left Bank #5: Borders & Boundaries

First edition, December 1993

Copyright © 1993 by Blue Heron Publishing, Inc.

ISBN 0-936085-58-4

ISSN 1056-7429

FOREWORD

I WAS DRIVING east, on vacation for the first time in several years, cutting through the Columbia River rimrock country near The Dalles at seventy-five miles-per-hour, humming a Jimmy Buffett tune. While I couldn't remember most of the words, the chorus began with "Changes in latitudes, changes in attitudes."

Incongruous as music from the wet Caribbean might seem in the parched West, to me it was appropriate. Within the space of a couple of hours, I had left western Oregon, traveled through the passageway of the Columbia Gorge — and entered a different world, dry where my home was wet, yellow where I knew green, empty compared to the populous Willamette Valley, peopled by folks of sun-squinted eye and more conservative political belief than those on the other side of the mountains. Should the world suddenly become rational, I thought, this country east of the Cascades would be an entirely different nation from that to the west. At the very least, it would be a different state.

Each of us is familiar with this phenomenon. Barriers, physical or not, exist all around us. Think of traveling and crossing an invisible line where everything is suddenly different, where people view the world through filters that do not exist for you. Think of meeting another human being so alien in appearance, manner, or language that understanding what he or she is thinking is well nigh impossible. Think of a conversation with a friend who suddenly reveals a belief so bizarre or mean-spirited that you are faced with reevaluating the very basis of your friendship.

Love and hatred, compassion and indifference, comfort and suffering, myth, language, symbolism, religion or irreligion, prosperity and poverty — all of these and more divide people as effectively as the Cascade Range sorts the Pacific Northwest into provinces of

5

mist and dust, coastal and continental, heavily populated and spaciously empty.

Given the improbability of entering another's skin, of experiencing another's thoughts and feelings, the walls between us are analogous to those tall mountains that back up the Pacific rains, giving our corner of the world its unique character. And since we are stuck with the mountains that divide us, whether we like it or not, it behooves us, if we ever wish to get along as a civilized world, to at least attempt to leave our own thoughts and feelings behind while trying to understand those of the alien other.

With these ideas on our minds, we selected materials for this, the fifth in our semiannual book series.

Sandra Scofield, Jennifer Mitton, Kathleen Tyau, Diana Abu-Jaber, and Christi Killien focus on family connections and disconnections. Poets William Stafford, Mary Misel, Mercedes Lawry, and Christopher Howell look at how and why barriers are crossed or aren't. Hollis Giammatteo writes of overcoming gender and class divisions, while David Suzuki reasons for checking human intervention in the natural world. Several of our authors write of political invention — James Aho on white paranoia, Ken Olsen on legal invasions, Robert Heilman on treasonous thought, Christopher Merrill on war. Others — Robert Sheckley, Mark Jarman, Robert Pyle — examine aspects of culture and personality in Paris, Los Angeles, and anymall U.S.A., while historian Richard White describes nation-building in an interview about the American West by Andy Helman. Larry Colton picks up on an aspect of that history through football and Indians. Michael Dorris and W. Ed Whitelaw deal with economic borders, the latter exhorting readers to distinguish between myth and reality using the Northwest economy as example. Cartoonist Matt Wuerker peers over bizarre edges, and artist Henk Pander draws on his World War II childhood in occupied Holland.

Now it's your turn to drive through the terrain. The first "changes in latitudes" we offer isn't the Caribbean but Hawaii. But forget your maps. Don't speed. Enjoy the scenery.

— Stephen J. Beard

ISLAND AND BEYOND

Kathleen Tyau

REMEMBER HOW YOU learned, when you were a child, how to find where you wanted to go and how to come back home? You learned what all the island people know, about how to go *mauka*, toward the mountains in the middle of the island, and how to go *makai*, toward the ocean lying all around. All other directions were marked by places you already knew how to find: Diamond Head, Pearl Harbor, Kaneohe Bay, Waianae.

How easy it was. When we got lost and our friends said, "Just go *mauka*," we went. When we were hungry, they gave us fish and poi. They invited us to come to their house for *kalua* pig and *lau lau*. We could bring our whole family, all our friends. We were never without laughter and love. There were always plenty of children running around. Your uncles played music and aunties danced the hula. Do you remember the bass your father, Kuhio played, with the string tied to the broomstick and stuck in a bucket of sand? We didn't even need a guitar in those days. We ate and sang the whole night long. We sang and talked story, just like I am now talking to you.

Do you remember the day your mama got lost? She was trying to find my house, here, up in Manoa Valley. I did not want to live *makai* anymore. Here I am safe from the tidal wave. Your mama stopped the car to ask an old man the way. *Mauka*, he said to her.

Just go *mauka* and you run into it. Which way *mauka*, you shouted out the window. Be quiet, your mama said, but you yelled and cried all the way to my house.

When you reached my house, you ran inside, shouting, Aunty, which way is *mauka*? Your mama thought you were being a smart aleck. She said you always asked too many questions and would not listen to what you were told. *Mauka* is toward the mountain, I told you. I know that, you said, but the last time we went *mauka* it was to Bobo's house on the other side of the island. How could *mauka* be in two different places? We laughed at you, but you were right. That is how I knew you would be leaving us someday.

How could you stay? The island *mauka* was not enough. You wouldn't go where the old man sent you. When we went to look at the house where you were born and the stream where the mullet ran and the graveyard where your grandmother and grandfather were buried, you wanted to know the names of the streets. You wanted to see the lines drawn on the map. What map? Nobody used maps. You were just a girl, but you had one. It was old and torn, but you took it everywhere you went. You were not content to stumble across what you were looking for. When you were only seven years old, you told me, Aunty, I am going to find Goong Goong. Which street goes *mauka* to heaven?

So you see, I was not surprised when you went away, when you went *makai* and *makai* and *makai*, way across the ocean, to the other side. You were looking for something, your own kind of *mauka*. I saw you go and I waited. I waited for you to come back, to knock on my door and say, Aunty, let me tell you what I know.

Now we sit and we talk, you, still young, and me, already old. I planted this banana grove when you were just a baby, and look at it now. I like to sit out here in the shade and feel the cool air. It is still quiet up here, except for the birds so loud in the morning. I hear them when I wake up, and I am glad we are both still alive.

We talk about the early days, before the freeways, when our family lived in Waikiki and we never locked our doors. In the summer we slept on the beach at Lanikai, and nobody asked us for a camping permit.

Do you remember driving *mauka*, over the old *Pali* highway, to get to the windward side of the island? Do you remember how the road wound along the cliff and everybody drove so slow? We could not go fast then, not like you can now when you take the freeway through the tunnel. But that was OK. We were not in a rush. We took our sweet time and we always got where we wanted to be.

On the *Pali* road the wind shook the car, and everyone got scared, except for you. When we stopped to look over the edge, you begged to climb on the rock wall. Your eyes burned like lava, fresh from the volcano. I knew *Pele* had gone inside your body, and she was talking for you. She was making you brave. I told your mama we should not make *Pele* mad, but your mama made you go back inside the car. Sometimes I ask myself, was it *Pele* who took you away?

Now you sit close to me and ask me how it was long ago — before Pearl Harbor, before you were born. I tell you about growing taro in the mud. I can still feel the mud on my feet, between my toes. It was so soft and warm, like walking in gravy. I tell you about picking *opihi* on the rocks, how we had to pick fast and then run on the rough coral before the waves washed us off. So many people died that way, but not us kids. We had tough feet, but I tell you, I was always scared. You ask me about your father's mother and my mother's mother, about what it was like when our family lived on Ni'ihau. But why do you not ask me, Aunty, which way is *mauka*? Why do you not ask me now, when I am finally ready to tell you?

Let me tell you a story that is mine, that I have never told you before.

I had a baby girl who died. Nobody talks about her anymore because they do not want to make me sad. She was my second child. When she was only a month old, she was *hanaied*, adopted by my family on Maui. I gave her to my parents because they were so lonely for me when I left for Honolulu. Her name was Leialoha. She was the lei of love I gave to my family. When she was only two years old, she died of influenza. She was gone before I could return to see her. In those days we could not fly back and forth between the islands like we can now. My heart was so broken, I did not go home until my papa died. When I finally returned to Maui, I searched for her bones. They said my papa had so much grief, he hid her bones in the old Hawaiian style. Nobody knew for sure where he laid her.

9

Some said *mauka*, up past the waterfalls, above the sacred pools of Kipahulu. Some said more *makai*, way beyond Kaupo. I did not know how far to go *mauka* or which way to go *makai*. I walked up and down the naked side of Haleakala until my feet had blisters. I walked along the ocean, on the lava path of the King's highway, crying "Leialoha, Leialoha," calling for my baby to come back, but the wind and the waves took my voice away.

I still dream about her. I have the same dream again and again. I know in my heart my baby is visiting me, even though she has your face. We are standing on the *Pali*, and I am holding her hand, only she turns into you, and you want to climb the rock. This is *mauka*, I say. Where we are now is *mauka*. Now let me go, you cry, so I do. I let you go and you jump off the cliff before I can stop you. But instead of falling, you turn into a bird and fly away. You fly *makai* and *makai* and *makai* until I cannot see you anymore. When I wake up, my face is all wet, not crying wet, but a soft kind of wet all over and through and through. My breasts, my arms, my legs are wet, as if I have been running through a cloud.

I do not tell you this to make you sad. When I wake up, I do not feel bad. All my pores have been drinking love. It does not matter that I could not find my daughter's bones. She still lives somewhere *mauka*, where I hold her close, and somewhere *makai*, where I let her go.

CUTTING MY HEART OUT: NOTES TOWARD A NOVEL

Sandra Scofield

T HERE IS A trigger in the woman's body, an impulse set off by
hormones as the baby comes to term. "It's time," it tells the
womb, and labor begins. Only it doesn't work in me; there is nothing that says, "Let go."

I carried my first baby ten months. I was on welfare; the staff at
the clinic assumed I was stupid. Nobody believed I was so over-
due. Nobody was concerned that, for weeks, I had been in pain, I
had been leaking. A friend who was a social worker took me to the
emergency room. She made a joke: "You've got belly power," she
said. "All you have to do is scream."

I screamed. Once I started — it was easier than I anticipated —
I could not stop. I screamed as they brought me a wheelchair, I
screamed on the elevator, I screamed until a nurse knelt in front of
me and said, We'll take care of you.

When your body doesn't do what it's supposed to do, they give
you a drug to start the contractions. They say it's like a skier on a

slope. Once you get going, you pick up speed on your own. Only I didn't. I don't.

For twenty hours they drip the drug into my IV. I am crazy with pain. Other women come and go. One, a black woman, says it's time, and they argue that it is not. Laughing, pushing, she wins, and has the baby in the labor room. Another woman shuffles in shackles; she has been brought from the county jail, accompanied by a matron and a male guard. They don't want to take off the chain. The resident yells (there is a lot of yelling in this room): How the hell do you think a baby will come out if the legs don't spread?

I wanted the baby. Not at first, maybe; not when I learned I was pregnant and didn't know if I could make it work with my lover. Not when I thought my life was drowning in a rain of trouble. But a baby fills you up and changes you from the inside. A baby makes you want it. You feel things, you get acquainted; there is somebody made from you. I did want him, but when they rolled me into the operating theater (instantly I understood why it is called that), and I looked up at the plate glass windows and saw interns and students filing in to watch, when I understood that I had messed this baby up somehow, with my bad luck, I was happy for the long needle in my spine, and happier still for the morphine lie that slid down my vein, past caring.

Later, I visited Baby. Before the birthing, he was perfect — handsome, robust, too robust for me to bear — and it was only the moments when he was locked in that changed that. The moments when he was caught, head out, by his shoulders, and there was no breath in him. The moments when he could not pass from me to the world.

When I was pregnant again, I knew better, and I was paying for my care. We made a date, the doctor and I, for January 2. No matter what.

On New Year's Eve my water breaks. My heart is thudding as I ride to the hospital in a cab (everyone has been drinking). They say I can come back later when labor starts, if I want. I start to cry. Read my chart, I say. Please. So they put me in a room to sleep, and in the morning they give me hard candy to suck. The candy contains the drug; contractions begin. This pain is different. This hospital is different. And I deserve this baby.

I will do everything right, I think. I will love her.

I wonder about details — feeding, burping, rashes and fevers (the baby book business has not yet boomed) — but it never crosses my mind that love itself is a commodity as questionable as aspirin, wine, sun, speed. There is too little, there is too much. Whatever you give, someone will say it was not the right amount. Someone will say you did not give it freely. You wanted it back.

IN FEBRUARY I flew to New York City to rescue my daughter, Jessica. She had fallen, not to crime or dissoluteness, but to hepatitis, and so I sat with her each day, horrified by her pale gauntness, tremors, and, most of all her rictal parody of a smile, brought on by Compazine and dehydration. At night I packed her things, clearing out the chaos and filth of her careless existence, boxing and taping and sputtering with exhausted tears. Yet I was happy. In the months she would be home, recovering, I would know where and how she was. We would not be separated. She would be safe.

WHEN SHE WAS fifteen, I picked her up at school one day. She was crying hard. A girl from her geography class had written her name in a toilet stall, she said. I made her wait in the car. I could not find anything. I told her not to worry. She was not sleeping through the night, nor eating. Her stomach hurt. She thought kids talked behind her back and all her teachers were unfair. She spent days in silence. I began sleeping in her narrow bed with her, so I would wake up when she did, so I could hold her if she wanted. One night she rose without disturbing me and ran a bath. I woke when I heard the water running out of the tub. I looked up, and in the moonlight I saw her standing in the doorway to the room. She was naked and wet. She sat down on the floor, dripping water, and I could not lift her, and she would not stand, and she did not speak, and after all the years when I had been so afraid for myself, waiting for my mother to show up from inside me, I saw it was in Jessica instead. If this can happen, I thought, anything can.

I don't read the newspaper. I watch the news on public television,

13

where larger issues merit time on the air. Elections, executions, earthquakes, wars. I don't watch violent movies. But I know what's out there. At night I have waked and felt a presence in the room. It's okay, I want to say. Stay here, I can take it. In the morning, I feel so foolish, to have assumed there is only one of whatever it is, and that I can tell it what to do.

I lived as a child in my grandmother's house in Wichita Falls, Texas. She had a neighbor whose house was like a great Southern mansion to us children. We dared one another to stick our feet across the property line. His house was white with columns, and it had a lawn like a putting green. He had once owned all the land around. He owned grocery stores in colored town. He shot a little kid — eight or nine — for playing on his yard one day at dusk, and he got by with it, because the boy was trespassing. I understood that this was how it was. Between my grandmother's house and the bus stop, I knew children whose fathers beat them with razor straps, and a girl who wasn't allowed to leave her house except to go to school or church. My own mother was crazy enough for shock treatments, pills, my family's constant eye, and, finally, early death. I grew up thinking it was Texas that gave my family so much bad luck. I could not wait to leave. Somehow, the burden my mother was had not eased when she died. My grandmother hoarded her few possessions and never spoke of her, and, I thought, watched me for signs of madness. I woke many nights from dreams I wanted to abandon. But I was an optimist then. I thought it was geography. I thought I could leave bad luck behind.

IN MAY JESSICA flies to Philadelphia to visit a new art school. I want her to like it. It is smaller, classical; going there is an act of faith in her talent (no computers, no illustration, no cartooning). I want her to believe in her future. Now the summer will yawn open in pure leisure. I have just completed a novel, and Jessica is well. Now, I imagine, we will talk. We will be close. I have the idea this will be the last of her summers here. She is twenty. When she was fifteen, and spent most of the summer in the hospital, she thought she and I were the same. She didn't think she had to tell me any-

thing, she says. She didn't know we were two people.

She calls from Manhattan. She has taken a room on Staten Island and a job as a foot messenger for a magazine she admires. She didn't intend to do this — she took only a single change of clothes — but, she says, she realized as she walked around Philadelphia, that it was time. She couldn't come home.

IN THE DAYS that follow, I lie on her bed in a kind of a wounded stupor. I tell myself what I have hold her a hundred times: that she will grow strong by acting as if she knew the way. And, little by little, my focus shifts from her to my mother. Over a course of days, I am so engulfed with memories and emotions, I can hardly stumble from one room to the other. It is as if my life has suddenly been compressed, moving from my own fifteenth year to this, my fiftieth, from one loss to the other, with nothing in between. I go back and forth in my mind.

EXCEPT FOR A few stories, I have always resisted the autobiographical impulse. I have thought my life not interesting enough, not intellectual enough, not rich enough in meaning, for fiction. Writing is an invention and an escape. It is about empathy and imagination. It isn't, is it, about me, after all?

I putter through my days. I write late, sometimes all night. I know in those hours that what I have lost, or never had, feeds my work. There is a chance to make things right, to find a new place where I have not been and did not know I wished to go.

15

IN THE COURSE of a few weeks, my next book arrives as if by mail, whole and demanding, in my mind. There we are, the summer after my mother died: my grandmother, my sister, my cousins and I, all of us in my aunt and uncle's home in Monahans. It is the summer I made a list of stories I would someday tell: stories about houses, about photographs, about quarrels, about secrets. Stories about sex (something adults did, to betray one another and their

children). I began writing, but with other stories, stories I thought of as fairy tales, stories that had not ever happened, stories about loss and fear, abandonment, and, in the end, safe haven.

I will shape that summer so that it is no longer what really happened. The "true story" does not have a clear narrative arc. The tensions are too muted. I borrow from something that happened when I was nine, something that happened when I was twenty. I fuss and muse and move into the fugue state in which I will write something I do not remember ever having known. This time, I think, I will let my mother go.

MY DAUGHTER DOES not get a phone. She does not give me an address. She arranges for Voice Mail, so I can leave messages. She checks several times a day. She calls when she has something to say. She has some good days, and some bad nights, she says, but I am not to worry. Really, she says, there is nothing you can do. Something cold slices through me. I remember how, after they plunged the needle into my spine, I had no more feeling below the waist. What can anyone give me for this, I wonder? What is the analgesic for cutting my heart out?

There is only one way I can accept this. "Do you mind," I ask her, "if I write about you in my new book? It's really about my mother, but with notes about you, too." I must let her draw the line, but I don't know what I will do if the boundary cuts through my vision.

She isn't especially interested. Impatiently, she says, "As long as you don't try to write what you think I'm thinking. As long as you stick to your own story."

And this I do, a little each day, pushing back the boundary that turns out to be inside me, not her, the wall between my safe haven and the story I have not wanted to tell. This I do, because, more than light or exercise or serotonin or even the love of my husband, writing saves my life. And in writing, Jessica, like my mother, is the stuff of fiction. I can make her what I will.

AFTERWARDS

William Stafford

Mostly you look back and say, "Well, OK. Things might have
been different, sure, and it's too bad, but look —
things happen like that, and you did what you could."
You go back and pick up the pieces. There's tomorrow.
There's that long bend in the river on the way
home. Fluffy bursts of milkweed are floating
through shafts of sunlight or disappearing where
trees reach out from their deep dark roots.

Maybe people have to go in and out of shadows
till they learn that floating, that immensity
waiting to receive whatever arrives with trust.
Maybe somebody has to explore what happens
when one of us wanders over near the edge
and falls for awhile. Maybe it was your turn.

"The domestication of the camel, not the invention of the wheel, liberated the early Arabs and allowed them to master the vast desert spaces and develop lucrative trade routes."

— James C. Simmons, "The Arabian Desert is No Place For Camels" in *Audubon*, January 1991 (Vol. 93, No. 1)

IN FLIGHT

Excerpt from the novel *Memories of Birth*

Diana Abu-Jaber

I WAS A baby at the time, maybe five years old. I remember walking and walking, movement without rest. We were crossing land whose name and nature were changing under our feet, part of a mosaic: the *nakbeh*, tragedy. I don't know how it was that we and the few women with us broke from the others, but we found ourselves following the boundary of the Jordan River, as if to delay our real departure — from native soil — as long as possible. I believe now that we were trapped in our own flight, as any species may be when they are dying: the raptors that refuse to mate, the American buffalo that lie down and will not eat. We might have been the last of our people for all we knew. We waded the hip-high grass of the riverbanks. Then, after perhaps a week of this wandering, we came to cutaway escarpments, shining bands of salt rimming the Dead Sea and freezing the earth.

At that place we crossed a wooden bridge that people would tell me later was not there, that it had been destroyed by Romans or Turks. They tell me, impossible, there has never been a bridge there. But it rises from memory in perfect clarity: stone joints, planked floor, grass stuffed between the cracks. We crossed from desolation into desolation, and when I turned to see where we had just come from, the bridge disappeared back into the landscape, and I felt the salt air fill my throat and mouth and etch into my heart.

We were not lost; that implies there was a way to go, a place to be lost from. We were homeless. We wandered at times in great circles. We tore the leaves from the trees to eat, and sometimes peeled the tender bark. I ate grass and dirt and winged beetles. As we walked away from the river we moved toward the desert, until the day we woke and it glittered under us in a plain of light, crystal white as the ocean.

That was the day the men found us. There were three of them on camels, swords tilted carelessly toward the sky, their animals drifting long, delicate legs under fur and rugs. The men were also wrapped up, heads bound in red and white. The desert stretched behind them, tufted with sparse grass, rock rising straight up in places like towers. They looked at us for what felt like a long time. I remember that long watching, their silence, that opal land, the white desert. A place that has never left my nights since then without some twist of dream.

"Here's some more," one man said.

The others nodded, as if they already knew us. In town we had called these sorts of men the *ruhhal*, wanderers.

The man touched his eyes then offered my mother his hand. "We ask respectfully that you come to live with us."

We followed them; sometimes I walked, other times I was carried upon a camel's undulating back. The land opened to us in cliffs and valleys, blue nooks and canyons. Their camp was hard to see through the yellow slant of sun. Light reflected from their sheep and the tents made of goat hairs, everything beaten to yellow. A black burro grazed by the edge of the grounds. Beyond that, we saw the shoulders of the *djebels* rising into the distance, folding mountains.

The *sitti*, matriarch of the tribe, emerged wreathed in black. Her face was tattooed over the chin, cheeks, and brow, and the eyes of the baby she held were blacked with kohl for the visitors. The other women came, and their arms were filled with leaves and flowers, as if they had known, perhaps even before we did, that we were coming, as if the desert floor murmured to them, bringing our footsteps over the land. They came, white veils lifting from their hair, arms filled, telling us, "Welcome, welcome, *assalamu alaikum*, you are home, at last, you are home again."

We lived with the Huwyatat Bedouins for a month. It was a time that my mother would later say was the happiest in her life, as if she had lived all her previous life with a chord tied about her waist. In the desert, the knot had broken and she went free.

"We know about the wanderings of marked men," said Sitti Jasmine. "For whom no land is home and against whom all hands are turned. Then there are nomads like us, who make the earth their home."

Jeneva, a woman who had come with us and had seen her home burned down, said, "You say that as if this desert *was* the whole world. You don't know what you're talking about. You don't know there are people out there, somewhere on the other side of the river right now, who will name your desert after their grandfathers, tell you that you never lived here, that the centuries were hallucinations, and that you will certainly never live here again."

One little girl said, "I'll take my daddy's pistol and shoot them!"

Sitti hushed her, gathering the child into her lap, and said to Jeneva, "If white-eyes come from all around to my desert, doesn't that prove my point? That this is land like any other on earth? When a man puts a name and draws his lines down on any piece of land, what foolishness. Those lines and words are invisible. Only in men's minds do these things exist. The Bedouin understand this. We walk and we know the joy in movement, in following the natural inclinations of the territory. We're content because the earth confirms that we're alive."

I remember a month of walking, of coming to campsites that dotted the earth, oases of stone walls and fountains, centuries stained. The Huwyatat would draw in their camel herds, set the black-haired sheets across the walls, and let the smell of coffee and cardamom rise, arabesques of smoke turning in the air. Sometimes we moved alongside an old railway line, where the camels wandered to graze between its tracks. We walked from *ouadi* to *ouadi*, the watering holes of valleys, muddy and flat in a white-scorched land or springing through green-terraced country. We carried embroidery, spun sheets and carpets, and listened to the clink of Roman coins and gold bands around the women's arms.

I also remember the absence in my mother's eyes as she gave herself to the march. The fact of movement and the company of others, I now believe, was what sustained her. Her eyes changed forever, imprinted with the image of a disappearing landscape, but I know the Bedouins gave something inviolable to us. In our first days of travel,

21

I saw an oasis that was like a lake; the water was vast, and as we came closer I saw that its surface was alive, that it moved and formed itself in pieces from the air. Then I realized that these pieces of lake and air were birds. Their wings shattered the air and their cries were layers of song, trebling, croaking, shrilling, musical and ornate, overlaid like the layers of Bedouin embroidery. That memory of bird song and flight was to return to me throughout my life.

The Bedouins lived lightly, leaving just the imprint of their feet, their gathering hands, and the camels' soft mouths to mark their passing. They were easy, too, with command, relying upon the elders, especially Sitti Jasmine, her skin brown as a tree stump and traced over. On the rare occasion that we met a visitor — once a falconer, another time, *journalists* from Britain — the men would cry out, *Alan wa sahlan!* Be twice welcomed! My tent, they said, is certainly your tent. And coffee, black, crude, and sugary, would be put before them. The falconer showed us how his bird sat on his leather glove, just a thread around the bird's talons and a tasseled hood over the bird's eyes like a too-large turban. The journalists had Sitti Jasmine speak into a whirring box. Their questions went round in circles, like men lost in the desert:

> Where do you travel?
> What do you eat?
> Where will you go next?

They pushed some buttons and we heard Sitti Jasmine's voice creak forth from under a cloud of whispery noises and repeat her answers. She clapped her hands together then and said in English, "You have jinnis in your boxes!" Then she turned to the rest of us and, grabbing her five-year-old granddaughter, said in Arabic, "But this one, big-ears, can repeat that trick in clearer voice and with extra commentary added in."

We came to a place that stretched beyond my mind's outlines: pillars, veined, footed, and engraved, some sunken almost completely in fields of yellow wild flower. There were stone-swept avenues that turned into plazas, stone altars, and theaters open to the air. We walked through carved archways, light-shot openings, where the men demonstrated how those before us had positioned weap-

ons or leaned out into the night, charting stars. The Huwyatat un-furled their carpets and moored them between pillars. Among the ruins, the smell of coffee was rich as earth.

From this place we passed single file, along ridges and between mountain crevices barely as wide as a camel's hips, places where the stone was hooked in a thousand places like piles of skulls, down a trail crusted in the earth. At the end of the trail we walked between the sides of two stone faces, set shoulder to shoulder. Siq, our leader's snow-white camel, swung its head back once, then we turned into a brilliant basin. Before us, pink and white, satiny as a girl's thigh, intricate as a heart, a facade emerged from the rock face.

I and the other children ran up before the riders to the beauty standing out of the rock. Its columns and archways were delicately hued as rose petals, and above those, atop the elaborate portico, there was an urn intricate as Aladdin's lamp. One of the men lev-eled his rifle at it.

"There's no gold in there, you fool," the leader said.

The other man put down his gun, shrugged, and said, "One never knows."

We walked along the clearing, and the leader pointed out other columns and openings, some just tracery along the rocks, sketches of palaces, others opened into rooms cut by shadows or dark and watery, swimming with bands of pink, blue, and ochre. Everything was silent, even the camels' feet seemed to walk in pools of silence. The dust in the air was still. The running children made no sound. Outside an archway, I found a fallen stone man; he had wild waves of hair and beard, empty eyes, and lips parted in silent command.

23

Birds skittered across the air, hectoring and wheeling. I stood by the toppled stone head and seemed to see time moving up the weathered stone walk. I ran to look for my mother and found her in the farthest room with her hand on the back of the leader's son, Ibn Abdel, the young man who had first found us. Her other hand was pressed between his shoulder blades as they sank down onto a rush mat. I quickly walked away.

We moved on again. One night we saw the silhouettes of riders on a *djebel* crest just ahead. Their cloaks unfurled like wings and we could see the black strokes of their rifles against the sky. I was terrified and began calling for my mother, only to have another woman tell me to hush. The children spoke of spirits, but one of the elders whispered, "No ghosts, unfortunately. These are only men."

Our men had begun shifting on their horses, taking the lead and unsheathing swords. We continued advancing as a group until they gestured for us to hang back. I felt my mother's hands encircle my waist.

A shot tore the sky from the crest over the length of the valley, then another, illuminating the rifle points. The Huwyatat men spurred their horses, their snake-limbed Arabs charging up the hillside, moonlight catching their flanks. The women stood and cried out, rippling their voices. They set up a ululation of war that rose, full and eerie as a ghost's lament, a ziggurat of sound.

We could see that our challengers were outnumbered. As the Huwyatat neared the hilltop, only a small band rode forward. The rifles had been used only to announce war, and the men drew swords that shone with the moon, blades clashing as we lost sight of the men in the dark. I remember flashes of metal, hooves, but most of all, I remember that keening song without words or end, with all the courage of a battle dance.

In the morning, the Huwyatat had taken the bodies of two challengers; the rest had been spared and fled. The men were from the Ahl el-Jabal tribe, enemies in a nearly forgotten blood feud, the women said. Other Huwyatat said the men were not lost but renegades, camel thieves, real criminals. Ibn Abdel came to me with a child's gold ring that he had found on the body of the man he had killed. "Perhaps this will fit you," he said. "This is probably from one of their young victims."

"Or perhaps it was a keepsake from his own child," another man said.

That night my mother tugged the ring off my finger and flung it into the sky.

Not long after that night my mother took me away from the other children. I had learned their games as well as their work, and I had learned to speak exactly as they did. My mother went to Ibn Abdel and said, "My daughter is getting to be savage like wild thorns, and this is not the kind of life I had hoped for her."

Sitti Jasmine, who also sat in the tent said, "It is exactly the kind of life she should have. She has fresh *leben* every day from the goat's milk, she learns the language of the desert wind and the paths of the stars. She has several grandmothers and grandfathers, many guides and protectors, playmates and cousins. She has daily contact with the beauty and health of animals, an understanding of mirages and visions, of Allah's munificent voice, of the bounty of spirit and the clean warmth of goat-hair blankets. Our life is the most perfect life, the most pleasing to God. So tell me, what sort of life is it that you had in mind for her?"

My mother squatted on the beaten floor, her brow tipped to her knees. At last she lifted her head and said, "This is not the life that *I* was born to. I can't keep moving like you. I need a place to stay in, even if it's a strange place. And I'm beginning to feel like I'll never be able to find myself again unless I stay still. I've been cut loose from my home and family. Sometimes I feel like my spirit has been lost over this desert of yours."

Ibn Abdel said, "I'm sorry, but for all of us. If you leave I will be losing a wife and daughter."

That week we came to an encampment, a collection of tents, corrugated metal, trash, wire. So different from the tidy camps of the Huwyatat, it looked as if it had been brought in and deposited by a circular wind. The eyes of the inhabitants were drops of lead that fell through me.

"The *mish ism*," the Huwyatat women murmured, "no names."

We gave them skins full of yoghurt, pistachios, figs, pressed apricot, and thyme, layer upon layer of the crackling leaves.

Ahlan, ahlan, they said, eyes lowered, peace be upon you, God bless you, bless your hand.

Through it all the Bedouins held their faces averted. The Huwyatat women made gestures against the evil eye and fingered the charms that dangled from their necks.

"We found them here last Ramadan," Ibn Abdel said. "Like you, wandering like baby goats, blind to the signs of the earth, sand and stars. These people were also separated the way you were. They were our first sign of the new white-eyes. But I talk too much. It is written, it is better to bless than to curse."

My mother held my hand, and we walked through the camp, through scraps of metal, a torn doll, the husks of food. Men squatted at their coffeepots over curds of black coffee, their clothes in tatters looking as if they'd shredded them with their own fingers. Their Arabic was shredded, the words flew into fragments of thought. I remembered the migratory birds at the first oasis we'd traveled to. I saw the torn wing of an ibis as it rose, low and uneven along the reeds, the movement of longing, dispersal, its cry the cry of dead souls.

The women clustered around us and talked about the taking of their village: soldiers marching in, doors and windows slamming open, bullets pinning corpses against buildings, men cut down at the knees, the sound of tanks. Those my mother and I saw at the camp had run for their lives, grabbing small possessions and running, and had come to this place, to Beit el Sala'am, they called it, to contemplate misery.

"Children died too?" I asked.

An old woman with the face of Sitti Jasmine grabbed my hand with both of hers. She was hurting me, but I couldn't pull away. "I had fourteen children!" she said. "Now they spin around the air above my head, trying to reenter my womb. I call to them, come back! They try to enter my ears and eyes and mouth, but there isn't room."

That night I slept in Sitti Jasmine's bed, and I dreamed of a man who looked familiar. He was calling my name, which broke into three parts.

This was how we began our life at Beit el Sala'am camp, and how I ended my life out of time with the Huwyatat Bedouin. I begged them not to leave us. And when it was time for them to go, Sitti Jasmine tried to hide me in one of the camels' back pouches. But Ibn Abdel came and returned me to my mother. For the short time I lived among the Bedou, I was lifted out of the stream of things and I saw how the earth, sky, and all things in it functioned together, each part of the world a part of the movement through and into it, and the movement of the Bedouin was the movement of the world, intrepid, caught in the winding tails of the spirits, the white, whipped edge of a sheet in the wind.

REFUGEE CAMP

Excerpts from *Rooms in the House of Stone*

Michael Dorris

WATER IS THE chief concern, several hundred miles to the south in Mutema. I'm in a car with Gerry Salole, the Ethiopian-born Save the Children Regional Director, and we stop to ask directions of Jonathan Bhizeki, the elected local Pump Minder, through a rolled-down window. Only five of the thirty-five deep wells and one of the fourteen bore holes for which he bears responsibility have water, he tells us, and even they are rapidly becoming exhausted. For the 12,000 people in and around this area of southeastern Zimbabwe, it's been a brutal, calamitous year. Not a single crop could be harvested, there is no food to buy in the shops, and no rain is expected until November. Handsome and distracted, Jonathan Bhizeki looks almost embarrassed, as if the sky's failure were his own.

Further up the road we visit the Chikwakwa Elementary School and talk with the principal. Dressed formally, as befits his position, in a tan tie beneath a maroon and white Argyle sweater, Clever Gwenzi is not hopeful. His father, born less than twenty kilometers away, has never in his lifetime seen such a drought. Economics eliminated the grade school children's lunch program, and as a result there are daily faintings and steep declines in attendance. It would cost an impossible 700 Zimbabwe dollars (about $140) each week to reinstitute a daily meal for all 423 students. Money is especially tight. The World Bank, anxious that the last vestiges of Zimbabwe's former inclination toward socialism be abandoned, successfully urged the imposition of a token tuition charge for all grade levels. Equivalent to one U.S. dollar per year per child, this fee constitutes a burden to the poorest families, who have responded by sending only boys to classes. Too many of the girls, Clever Gwenzi regrets to say, have resorted to prostitution in order to eat.

As we drive up the hill away from Chikwakwa, we experience a small miracle: a two-minute rain shower. It's so surprising Gerry stops the car and turns on the windshield wipers. Nothing happens. Though the odometer shows in excess of 60,000 miles driven, no previous driver has had occasion to realize that the wipers are not connected.

The rain stops as quickly as it began, and a moment later there's no evidence it ever happened — no puddles, no glistening surfaces. The land is so dry, it has instantly inhaled every drop of moisture.

Our last stop is the community clinic, a rectangular cinder-block structure with a commanding view of the valley below and home to a resident physician and three nurses. The building shares a single well with the educational compound — and now with much of the general population. If that well fails, the doctor tells us, everything will close down within a day's time.

"How is the general health of the area?" Gerry inquires. Save the Children has operated here in the Middle Sabe region for many years and has in fact contributed heavily to the construction of many of the newer buildings. There is, consequently, a particular responsibility, a special relationship. There is an unsubstantiated rumor that villages with an established bond to an international charity are at a greater than usual risk during hard times because the government, fully expecting that they will be assisted by enhanced donations from abroad, moves them down on the priority list of needy domestic cases. Unfortunately, Western philanthropic donations generally have dropped rather than increased — a phenomenon professional fund raisers term "famine fatigue" — and the expectations of dependent communities are impossible to meet.

The health-care workers seem exhausted, defensive. They describe protein deficiency, pellagra, but vehemently deny having seen any cases of AIDS. Just send the medicine we require, they tell us. We'll take care of things from there. In the dazzling African sunset, the stark white buildings stand in relief against a red-orange, cloud-less sky, and not even the sound of birds intrudes upon the silence. There's a dying tree in the center of a circle of stones, a gesture toward landscaping. To change the subject, I ask the species, but no one knows. It's not indigenous.

"I had a farm in Africa," Gerry Salole quotes from Isak Dinesen, and I quite understand the literary allusion. The romantic, European-viewed Africa of stampeding herds of wildebeest, endless frontier, and solitude is seductive, much gentler than the parched bed of the Sabe River, studded with the decaying carcasses of animals who came to drink and found no moisture.

TO A NEW arrival, "camp" must seem a bizarre designation for Tongogara, a colonial plantation turned refugee center near the eastern Zimbabwe border where 42,000 displaced Mozambicans wait behind a steel fence — some since the mid-1980s — for their particularly vicious civil war to wind down. Every moving vehicle, every running child, is announced by a trail of the fine bronze dust that eventually coats everyone and everything with the same earthy skin.

This place, described to me as "the Hilton Hotel of Refugee Camps," is a grid of red-orange mud-and-thatch huts, schools, and bureaucracy. It's efficiently, if somewhat dictatorially, run by David Malambo, a corpulent administrator who wears three college rings, a chronometer watch, a cowboy shirt with snaps instead of buttons, and an ornate Texas belt buckle. He presides from an office decorated with thirty-three hand-printed aphorisms, inspirational sayings such as, "I am blessed and I confer blessings on others." I sit before his huge desk, blasted by his wide, constant smile and booming laugh, while his shrewd, intelligent eyes, belying the more clownish aspects of his public persona, fix me to my chair.

I listen, spellbound, as David Malambo unfolds one enormous hand and with the other, counts off his NGO wish list, finger by finger. His top priority, along with the drilling of additional wells, is the installation of a camp-wide loudspeaker system so that his frequent announcements will be instantly accessible to all residents,

direct and without the confusion of reinterpretation. The donations he seeks from Western donors range from vials of sulfa drugs to a basketball ("for the 22,000 children") to a renewal of his personal subscription to *National Geographic*.

Recently the camp almost had its first full-time doctor: a Hindu from India, trained in Great Britain, was willing to come, but the appointment fell through. It does boast a brand new Dewey-decimal-driven library, built with Italian lira that houses, between the "Silence" signs, books like *The Economic History of Canada* and seventeen copies of an introductory calculus paperback published in 1978. The collection, in general, easily replicates the back-room bookshelves of half the people I know: once-used college textbooks, old issues of *Time* magazine, Sharper Image catalogues whose high-tech gadgetry in this desperate African context must seem the far-fetched stuff of science fiction.

For years now, the stream of refugees has continued to flow through the gates: hungry, worn-out, disheartened people, struggling across the parched landscape of a Road Warrior film. Each person has a story, as tragic and archetypal at its heart as an epic novel: the search for a lost son or daughter; widows, unaccompanied orphans, some too young to relate any information about themselves beyond a nickname. When there's film, their mug-shot photographs are distributed throughout the camp in hopes that someone, somewhere, will recognize a face.

Within sight of the former owner's swimming pool, now padlocked and dry, today's cluster of displaced persons sit dazed on  packed dirt, "guarded" by a contingent of bored soldiers. Most speak a dialect related to Shona, the predominant tribal language of Zimbabwe, and so I'm able to communicate through Mark Nyahada.

He's come to Tongogara today to supervise a newly inaugurated program, run cooperatively by Save the Children, the Zimbabwe government, and a U.S. team of psychologists and social workers from Duke University, aimed both at reuniting separated family members and caring for the youngest witnesses to unspeakable violence.

"Some of these children," Mark tells me in his very British accent, "have seen terrible things. They've been forced to kill their parents. Made to carry ammunition across enemy lines. Seen people locked inside houses that were then set on fire."

In the late-morning torpor of the reception area, where the only sounds are the buzz of flies and the low conversation of soldiers, it's hard to imagine such atrocities — until I see the eyes of one little boy about ten years old. His expression is exhausted, devoid of curiosity, matching the listlessness of the elderly woman beside him.

Mark notices the direction of my gaze. "That's his grandmother," he tells me. "His mother is still somewhere in Mozambique. They hoped the father would be here, but so far we haven't been able to locate him."

Mark beckons, and the boy comes over, joins us, and in the custom of men conversing, we squat face-to-face. Unmoving, the grandmother stares through us as if watching another place and time. There are stretched holes in the lobes of her ears where jewelry once dangled. Mark estimates that she's no more than fifty, and yet she appears to me much older.

There's nothing childlike about this boy, nothing playful or energetic. Like so many people I will meet in these camps, he has about him an air of distilled dignity, as if, denied every other possession, he has quietly retained possession of himself.

Mark translates the story the boy elects to tell us, and it is, within this inhumane context, undramatic, even typical. Yes, he's gone days without eating. Yes, he and his grandmother have walked shoeless from a long distance. Yes, he's hoping to find his father, who ran away from their village some time ago to avoid execution for being the brother-in-law of the wrong person. The boy is neither rushed nor especially interested, just tired. He's never been to school, but clearly he's intelligent, a survivor. If it weren't for his size, for the absence of lines on his face, I'd think I was in the presence of a resigned, mature man.

Mark promises that he'll circulate the boy's photograph throughout the several refugee centers scattered along the frontier; he'll even send it along to his counterpart in Malawi, where more than one million Mozambicans have fled. Perhaps a relative will see it and contact the authorities. Perhaps the story will have a benign resolution.

The boy nods, then rejoins his grandmother. Mark and I stand, brush off our knees, and walk towards our Toyota. We're running

31

behind schedule, late for a meeting. Before I get into the car, however, I turn back for one last look. The boy is cradled in his grandmother's thin arms. His mouth is at her empty breast.

Bad luck has created this predicament, bad luck and the incessant meddling of foreign governments — who've lost interest in Southern Africa now that the cold war is history. At one end of the looping line of connection is pain, and at the other is carefree joy. At the far extreme stands that prematurely old little boy of Tongogara. A million options and possibilities away are we, am I. Thrown together by arbitrary chance at an arbitrary moment in time, we found ourselves occupying the same place — we beheld each other, registered our similarities. For every child like him, there are 100,000 more I don't happen to encounter, and for every man like me, there are millions he can't imagine, yet we stare across the chasm, try briefly to fathom the other's life.

No greater distance separates us than this: he stays, I leave. But not entirely alone. I have a daughter about his age, a shining girl whose last act before my trip was to empty her bulldog bank and send her birthday money along for me to give away. To her, on some unspoiled level, she and the boy I've just met have the obvious potential of contemporaries, of playmates. She has not yet learned to tolerate injustice as inevitable, to become defeated in advance by the enormous odds against making a difference by reaching out. For her, what's directly before her eyes is still visible, and the equation is quite simple. They, need, I have. Therefore, I give, in order to reestablish a fair balance.

As Mark and I drive north on a two-lane road, past grass-roofed villages and straggling goats that seem more bone than flesh, the faces of two children — who will never meet — superimpose and fix permanently in my imagination.

ANOTHER TIME: A JOURNEY TO KOSOVO

Christopher Merrill

P RISTINA, THE CAPITAL of Kosovo and, many Western diplomats
fear, the next target of Serbian aggression in the Balkans, is a
dingy, unfinished city. Dust swirls through vacant lots, the streets are
teeming with unemployed men and women, and MIG fighter jets
scream overhead. Although the population of rump Yugoslavia's
southern province is 90 percent ethnic Albanian, the Serbian minority is in complete control. Countless Albanians have lost their jobs to
Serbs: the Grand Hotel, for example, once the city's pride, is now
staffed by Serbs; Albanians are no longer permitted to enter. Outside,
Serbian militiamen do not sling their automatic weapons over their
shoulders but walk instead with their fingers on the triggers.

"Kosovo," a friend had said before I left for Pristina, "is a massa-
cre waiting to happen."

This has been disputed land for a long time. It was in 1389 that
the Turks defeated the Serbs here, ushering in 500 years of Otto-
man rule — a decisive battle that then became the subject of Serbian
mythology. Experts call Serbian President Slobodan Milosovic's
speech on the 600th anniversary of that defeat a turning point in
the rise of the "Greater Serbia" movement, which has fueled so much

33

hatred and fighting in Bosnia. Preying on nationalist sentiments, so the argument runs, the Serbian leader created a climate suitable for the next campaign of "ethnic cleansing." Kosovo is Yugoslavia's — and, indeed, the international community's — dirty little secret: here is Europe's version of apartheid. The Albanian schools are closed, the media are in the hands of the Serbs, and what Albanian political leaders call a systematic program of terror under the guise of direct — i.e. Serbian military — rule is underway.

Under the terms of the 1974 Yugoslav constitution, Kosovo was an autonomous province until Serbian authorities revoked that status in 1989. Two years later, in an unauthorized referendum, Kosovoans voted for independence, and last year they elected a president and regional assembly — to no avail. Now diplomats fear that if and when peace comes to Bosnia, the Serbs will turn their attention to Kosovo, and the Albanians will be slaughtered. "It would take the Serbs forty-eight hours to overrun Kosovo," said a diplomat who spoke on condition of anonymity. "And Milosovic knows no one will stop him."

Yet if it is true that the West will not intervene, it is also quite possible that Kosovo's neighbors will not stand idly by. Albania may defend its fellow Illyrians, and it is not difficult to imagine other countries — Greece, Bulgaria, Turkey, and even Russia — taking advantage of the fighting to start another Balkan War. Meanwhile, the Serbs are provoking the Kosovoans, according to some observers, in order to spark enough unrest to justify their own invasion of the province. The key to maintaining peace here, at least in the short run, lies in the ability of the leadership of the Albanian League for Democratic Kosovo to convince its party members not to strike back.

A tall order.

"Ask a cab driver to take you to the headquarters of LDK," a British filmmaker had told me in Belgrade. "If he's Albanian, he'll take you there and introduce you to everyone you need to know. If he's Serb, you might end up in jail."

My cab driver was, in fact, Serbian, but since he was suffering from emphysema and seemed to need my money more than the chance to preserve his honor, he drove me, albeit with a sneer, to a small Quonset hut behind the soccer stadium. Here was as well the

Albanian PEN Center, and inside I met a number of writers, artists, intellectuals, and politicians.

"These are the only free fifty square meters in Kosovo," said a man who had taught linguistics at the local university until the Serbs had fired him and his colleagues, "so everyone comes here." He pointed toward the ceiling. "Of course the place is bugged, but we don't care if they listen to us here."

I was struck immediately by the various languages spoken around the main table — Albanian, English, French, and German. Weeks earlier, in Zagreb, I had asked a Croatian art critic to explain the stereotypes underlying the different ethnic jokes of the region. "Serbs are nasty," she had been quick to say, "Croatians are clean, Slovenes orderly, Bosnians stupid, and Albanians can't learn languages." The language Albanians cannot, or will not learn, I realized, is Serbo-Croatian — the language, that is, forced on them by the authorities. Theirs is a Romance language, a far cry from a Slavic tongue, and it is no wonder that they insist on speaking, conducting business, and educating their young in their familiar way. Thus they have set up parallel institutions — private schools, clinics, and businesses — in an effort to preserve their traditions, a situation that does not sit well with the authorities. A dental surgeon led three of his students into the room, two young men and a women who had just been arrested for studying in Albanian. They had been beaten on their hands, and they were terrified.

"They were coming to my clinic to get their grades," said the dentist. "These kinds of things happen every day."

Another man, thirty or so, shuffled in, plump, soft-eyed, and soft-handed. His eyes were bloodshot, and he needed a shave. I wondered for a moment if he might be hungover. No. For five hours the previous night he had been beaten, threatened, and brutally interrogated by a pair of drunken militiamen. His crime? Selling videos of Albanian folk dances. His captors had cocked a pistol in his mouth for an interminable length of time, shouting over and over that he was a dead man. It was a miracle, he believed, that they had not shot him. Now they had given him ten days to leave town. Where would he go? I wondered.

"Where can I go?" he asked. "They don't let us have passports."

35

Did I want to see his bruises? a doctor asked me. I nodded — a decision I soon regretted. Never had I seen such deep bruises and welts, purple masses covering his shoulder blades, upper arms, and buttocks. "We think his right hand is broken," the doctor concluded, "but we can't get any X rays to be sure."

I was aghast. Why had he shaken my hand? I could not say. Had I gripped his firmly? I could not remember.

My next stop was the office of the Committee for Rights and Freedom, where I interviewed Hydajet Hyseni, a poet and journalist who had spent ten years — almost the whole of his adult life — in prison for "dissident activities." He had spent so much time behind bars, I learned, that he had not been able to study English, and he apologized for having to use a translator — a kind, elderly gentleman who had been a banker, had even secured multimillion-dollar loans from the World Bank, before he and the other Albanians working with him had been fired. It occurred to me that in another time a poet and a banker might not have much to say to each other. Not so now. These men seemed close, and I was moved as much by the way in which fate had brought them together as by Hydajet's descriptions of his arrests for "illegally" publishing poems and organizing demonstrations, of torture and solitary confinement in prison, of his determination to document Serbian abuses and provocations without succumbing to the temptation to retaliate. Then he showed me enough photographs of murdered and mutilated civilians to turn my stomach, and when it was time for me to leave I was shaking.

"I hope the next time we meet," he said, "we can talk about poetry." And the banker suggested that on my next visit I stay with him. "There are war criminals in the Grand Hotel," he said. "You don't want to stay there."

I was too rattled to return to my room, and so I walked around the city, trying to collect my thoughts. I was frightened, yes, but not for myself. I knew that I could board a bus to Macedonia, where I could buy a plane ticket away from there. The Albanians were not so fortunate, is what I was thinking when at sunset I came to a plaza, in the middle of which was a tall, tri-pronged white monument. Suddenly the sky was full of black birds, thousands and thousands of birds circling the monument. It was a strange moment, which filled me with dread.

I walked off, only to come back minutes later. I had to learn the name of the monument. By now the birds had settled on the roofs of the nearby apartment buildings, and I looked around for someone who might speak English. Off to the side was a handsome couple. I approached them, and it was not until I had spoken to them that I noticed the man was wearing a beard — a sign in these parts of a Serbian Chetnik. What was more, on his jacket was the "greater Serbia" insignia. I should have begged their pardon and walked away. Instead, I asked them what the monument was called. The man said something in a pleasant voice. "What does that mean?" I asked. "Togetherness," he said. "The three cultures?" I said. "Muslim, Catholic, and Orthodox?" "Yes," he said. Then I asked him if he would write down the name in my notebook, and as I flipped through the pages I realized that among the loose papers falling out were lists of murdered and missing Albanians. My heart was pounding, but I kept going until I found a blank page. When he had written out a name I could not read, I thanked him.

"Another time," he said, meaning, I presume, "Any time."

Under the circumstances his slip seemed more than appropriate.

37

IF AT FIRST YOU DON'T SECEDE...

Robert Heilman

ISINCERELY BELIEVE that the breakup of the American West into smaller states is desirable and inevitable. I realize that probably seems outlandish, but then, unless you live here, you are an outlander and can't be expected to understand.

Although it is acceptable, even fashionable these days, to talk about the breakup of the Soviet Union in terms of the dissolution of the old Russian Empire, to speak about the same process occurring here in the United States is seen as eccentric, if not — alas! — treasonable.

It's too bad that we haven't the language for this kind of discussion, because the problems are real enough and the approach is straightforward and reasonable. But the vocabulary just isn't there, and so the notion seems silly because of the language it's couched in. You run the risk of either falling into crackpot secessionism or hopelessly abstract pedantry. It is terribly difficult to speak of redressing the very real problems of a particular area through geopolitical realignment without seeming, well, provincial in your outlook.

With the growth of communications technology and the increasing interweaving of large-scale economic, political, and environmental concerns we've heard a great deal about a developing global community. Yet, for all its intellectual appeal, the Global Village cannot be lived in like a real town.

38

People care about what they can see with their own eyes and understand in their hearts. The world we walk through and work in is our real world. Beyond that daily experienced world we can have no effective allegiance, we can do no useful work, because we can only harm whatever we touch but don't understand.

MY ANCESTORS HAD a word, *heimat*, that expressed it as well as it could be expressed. It's usually translated as "homeland," the nearest English equivalent, but it means much more than just a location.

It includes not only the place but the land itself, the people who live there, and their ways of doing things. It includes the great cycles of the seasons, the weather, the animals wild and domestic, the towns and the houses in those towns and the people who live in them and their kinships and traditions, all the long list of relationships we find in Ecclesiastes 3:1-8, which begins, "For everything there is a season and a time for every purpose under heaven." It is a concept that is all-encompassing in terms of time and ecology and culture but limited to a particular place.

Due to a series of calamities beginning in November 1793 my family has spent 200 years in a generations-long search for *heimat*. Through all these migrations it has been the changing times that forced us to move more than the place. Good land is surely enough for anybody, but the shifting of politics with the resultant wars and famines and economic troubles made the good places dangerous. In each case the changes did not come from within the place and in response to the local needs but from elsewhere — Paris, Vienna, Moscow, and Washington D.C. — and to serve outside needs.

The history of my own family, then, is the history of the destruction of our *heimat* by political, economic, and cultural forces that see our homes in terms of their own needs and not in terms of our needs.

Of course, we're speaking here about imperialism. But that's a worn-out, nearly meaningless word, the sort of cliché that's sure to keep whatever you have to say from being taken seriously. It is better simply to call it what it is: the destructive exploitation of groups

39

of people and the places where they live by more powerful outside groups.

MY *HEIMAT* IS the Umpqua valleys, part of the State of Jefferson, that mythical (since you won't find it on any map) but very real (since I and my neighbors actually live here) mountainous region consisting of the Klamath, Rogue, and Umpqua basins and their associated coastal streams.

Politically, you can define it as the twelve counties of Douglas, Coos, Curry, Josephine, Jackson, and Klamath in southwestern Oregon and Modoc, Siskiyou, Del Norte, Shasta, Trinity, and Humboldt in northwestern California.

It's an area roughly the size of Wales or Brittany, with a population of 700,000. It is arguably the wealthiest region of the West Coast in terms of natural resources such as timber, fish, gold, and other minerals. It is also probably the most poverty-stricken, the Appalachia of the West Coast.

People here understand clearly that the region, which is culturally and physically a whole, suffers from having been divided by an arbitrary line, forty-two degrees north latitude, back in 1850.

IN THE HEADLONG rush of Manifest Destiny the terra incognita of the West was carved up into huge blocks based on sextant readings rather than landscape. The eastern United States had a 160-year period of settlement, plenty of time to appreciate the differences between natural regions.

Take a look at a map of the United States and you'll find the right-hand side crowded with little places with jagged boundaries. By contrast, we have counties here in the West that are larger than most of the New England states. The American West, that "trackless waste" on the left, is an exercise in Euclidean geometry, reflecting the ignorance of policy makers far removed from the land who treated it as if it were as undifferentiated as the ocean, to which they, in fact, often compared it.

But real differences based on the physical lay of the land exist and have always existed and will continue to exist, despite legislative ignorance. They are immediately apparent to anyone with eyes to see.

As early as 1852, the people of my region understood the consequences of this false line and petitioned the government in Sacramento for the creation of the State of Shasta. It died in committee, of course, so they tried again in 1853, asking for the State of Klamath. In 1854, they gathered in Jacksonville, Oregon Territory, to try to form the State of Jackson. The advent of the Civil War brought on new efforts, this time to secede not only from Oregon and California but from the Union as well.

If at first you don't secede, try, try again. In the 1890s a movement toward a State of Jefferson began. By 1941 the movement had gained enough support that the region formally seceded from the States of California and Oregon.

On Thursday, December 4, 1941, Judge John Childs of Crescent City was elected governor of Jefferson at a meeting held in Yreka. The new state adopted a great seal depicting a symbolic double cross on a gold pan. Roadblocks were set up and pamphlets were handed out to motorists welcoming them to "the Forty-ninth State." Three days later the Japanese bombed Pearl Harbor. On Monday, December 8, Judge Childs declared war on Oregon, California, and Japan and then dissolved the new government.

In the mid-1980s a coalition of Greens, no-nukers, anarcho-syndicalists, organic farmers, New Age neo-pagans, eco-feminists, and sociology professors began to put forth a social, economic, and political theory called "bioregionalism." The notion (which, despite the unwieldy name, was quite simple) was to bring a host of single-issue groups together by focusing on the effects of all their many concerns on a particular place.

Under the sociopolitical rubrics of "deep ecology," "sustainability," "reinhabitation," "holistic approaches," and "decentralization," the coalition reinvented the wheel, and, dubbing our home valleys the Klamath-Siskiyou Bioregion, called for the establishment of a leftist utopia. The movement never caught on outside of the counterculture though, perhaps because of its failure to include the region's conservative majority in its definition of "us."

It's too bad that the bioregionalists aren't much of a force around here anymore. In many ways, despite their hopelessly abstract rhetoric, the underlying principles they hold are really worth considering.

It takes a good long while for an essentially European culture to adapt to the American West. Particular places have particular needs, and we ignore local conditions only at great risk to our ability to survive. We need more than just a healthy national (or worse yet, international) economy and culture. We need thriving local ones as well.

THE STATE OF Jefferson is an idea that refuses to die. The region is still secessionist in outlook. The name lives on in businesses such as the Jefferson Bank and National Public Radio affiliate network Jefferson Public Radio of Ashland, Oregon. From time to time editorials supporting or opposing the notion appear in local papers.

The idea lives on because, like the Kurds, we are a people without sovereignty, and we suffer culturally, politically, and economically, from our lack of control over our own destiny.

The legislative decisions that affect our lives are never made here. They are made in Salem and Sacramento and Washington D.C., where we are not heard because our voice is drowned out by the more numerous and more powerful urban flatlanders to the north and the south and the east.

As a region, we have no balance of trade deficit with foreign nations because we are overwhelmingly net exporters of raw materials. We generate millions of dollars more in taxes and other government revenues than we receive. Our land base is almost entirely controlled by federal and state governments and multinational corporations. It is not much of an exaggeration to compare the region to a third world country.

The economic life of our communities is dominated by corporations whose headquarters are elsewhere. The capital generated by outside interests operating here flows out of the region at a much greater rate than their local investments and helps fuel the stock exchanges and real estate markets of Tokyo, Hong Kong, New York, Seattle, Portland, and San Francisco. Yet our per capita income and

42

employment levels are significantly lower than state and national averages, and our emergency food use and infant mortality rates are higher.

We live under two different sets of state laws though we are one people. A few months before the onset of the Reagan error "trickle down" recession of the early 1980s, the Oregon Legislature passed a welfare reform act denying benefits to two-parent families. This experiment in conservative social engineering forced some 300 southern Oregon families to cross the border into northern California where, though the unemployment rates were just as high, they were eligible for assistance.

THOMAS JEFFERSON CLEARLY understood that *e pluribus unum* was not just an end but an equation, for the one is really many. Here in the State of Jefferson, where, despite the pressures, the rural-centered ideal of Jeffersonian democracy is not an antique notion but our way of life, that way is in danger of dying out, suffocating under the pressure of outside concerns that ignore our own needs.

Is political and cultural diversity a threat to the Union? Only when it is frustrated and ignored. I prefer to think of it as a source of strength. Of course, Oregon and California would be poorer without us, but we would be richer without them. The United States would be richer too if our voice was given equal weight with theirs.

WE'RE UNCOMFORTABLE CALLING OURSELVES IMPERIALISTS

AN INTERVIEW WITH RICHARD WHITE

Andy Helman

IF YOU SAW Richard White, McClelland Professor of History at the University of Washington, it would come as no great surprise that his specialty is the history of the American West. He might very well have stepped right out of Buffalo Bill's Wild West Show. Or, for that matter, he might be that long-locked, silver-haired gentleman himself. White, author of It's Your Misfortune and None of My Own: A

New History of the American West, *is a "new West historian," one of a select few historians with revisionist — some would say simply realistic — views on the settling of the American West, the mythologies of the pioneers, the treatment of American Indians, and forest ecology, among other things.*

An Easterner who landed in Seattle via California and Utah, White has garnered numerous honors, awards, and fellowships. The topics he has covered range from ecological issues to outlaw gangs to race relations in the American West. As a consultant, White has been an expert witness for the Puyallup Indian Tribe, as well as an advisor to the Public Broadcasting System and the British Broadcasting Corporation.

Andy Helman: You have said that the federal government created itself in the West. What did you mean by that?

Richard White: One of the things to remember about American history is that the American state was very weak for much of the nineteenth century. Only in the West, where the territories were even weaker, did the federal government have room to expand. To draw a metaphor, the West was the kindergarten of the American state, a place where the government could try things out. It was in the West that the first bureaucracies outside of the post office began to grow up — the Land Office, the Indian Bureau, the U.S. Geological Survey. It was in the West that the government took a major role in supplying capital for development, as it did for the Transcontinental Railroad and as it did during World War II with the defense industry. Look at California today, as federal money is pulled out of the defense industries, and you begin to get a gauge of how important the government has been, even in one of the most politically powerful sections of the nation. Look where we are, in the Pacific Northwest. The electricity running your tape recorder comes from federal dams on the Columbia River. We could go on and on and on in this vein.

What the West provided the federal government was an arena where it could do things it would later do elsewhere in the United States. But it is important to note that here, it did those things without much opposition. Westerners tend to forget that they begged the government to conquer the Indians, set up military bases, build dams.

AH: In your book you say, "Westerners usually regarded the federal government much as we would regard a particularly scratchy wool shirt in the winter. It was all that was keeping them warm, but it still irritated them." When you said that, what period were you talking about? Then? Or then and now?

RW: I'd say it's a trait that continues to distinguish Westerners. What irritates Westerners is that they can only get the capital they need through a powerful federal government, but while they want a government powerful enough to help, they don't want a government that asserts any sort of control over the resources it provides. That has been characteristic of the West throughout its history. The people who have gotten the biggest subsidies in the United States are in the West. Look at the ranchers, who have once again succeeded in vetoing increased grazing fees on public lands. Now you can argue about whether low grazing fees are for the better or the worse, but they do represent a subsidy for this particular group, Western ranchers. At the same time, there is no group I know of that sees itself as supreme individualists more than Western ranchers.

AH: And yet this strong vision of the Westerner as the rugged individualist remains. And you say it began even before the West was settled. How did that happen?

RW: The sense that the future lay in the West is older than American culture. In European society, even before the discovery of America, there was the sense that to go West was to meet the future. Actually going West, as Americans did in the nineteenth century, however, involved practicing a form of self-deception. For the West to be what the pioneers wanted, it had to be emptied; anyone who was already there had not to matter. Americans moving West practiced this incredible sort of egotism. Because they were going to redo it, because all they saw were the possibilities of their own particular futures, what happened to Indians didn't matter. Indians were the past, whites were the future. In the Southwest, same thing, Mexicans were the past, whites were the future.

What's interesting about the West today is that people who used to see themselves as the future are beginning to see themselves as the past. Rural Westerners, who for so long thought their way of life was the future and that the future was on their side, now feel besieged — and rightfully so. They are making comparisons be-

46

tween themselves and the Indians, a comparison many Indians find both ironic and not particularly convincing. You find the same sense of being besieged in the Southwest, there by illegal immigrants — which really is astonishing! The majority of the people living in the Southwest today arrived after World War II, and yet there is virtual hysteria over the migration of people from Mexico — or even from other parts of the United States. If you live there, the uproar seems to make sense, but step outside the area and none of it makes much sense. It's as if people have no perspective on their own experience.

AH: So you don't believe there should be boundaries?

RW: Well, there are boundaries. It's not my job to decide whether there *should* be boundaries. I'm a historian; my job is to point out certain realities about those boundaries. And one of the realities about the boundary between the United States and Mexico is that it has been virtually impossible to enforce since it was set back in the nineteenth century. This idea that we are going somehow to seal the border to Mexico? Frankly, I think unless people are willing to put the Army along that border and pay the huge expense needed to keep it there, people will continue to come across.

AH: When people speak of the "imagined West" — are there different versions of the imagined West?

RW: Well, I'm doing an exhibit on the imagined West at the Newberry Library. And to show you what I mean, around the corner from the Newberry is a Thai restaurant. As you go in, there is a picture of a four-year-old Thai kid dressed up in a U.S. Cavalry outfit. And he's saying, "Hello, my name is Amaret. I'm an American. I love Thai food." How does Amaret show he's an American? He shows he's an American by dressing the part. The point is that people literally imagine the part for themselves.

Historically, Americans have imagined the West in two very different ways. One was that the West was empty, that there were a few Indians, but they were dying out and would retreat before white people. This made the West a place waiting for white America to take over. This was Turner's frontier, the frontier where people willing to work hard and make their own life could come and by the sweat of their brow build a good life for themselves.

47

AH: By Turner, you mean...?

RW: Frederick Jackson Turner. He wrote of the significance of the frontier in American history.

The other imagined West is best shown by Buffalo Bill. Buffalo Bill's West wasn't empty. It was full of Indians. And it was not going to be peacefully occupied like Turner's frontier; it was going to be occupied by killing people, in a bloody, violent conquest of the Indians. It was a land bought with blood, a land where the farmer is not the hero, but rather the scout.

An interesting thing about this second imagined West is that Americans have a hard time admitting they conquered the place. And one of the fascinating things about the conquest is that it may be the only conquest in history in which the most celebrated military actions were defeats. And not just defeats, but defeats in which people were killed to the last man. Ask people to name two famous battles that took place in the American West, and almost universally, their answers will be Custer's Last Stand — we lost — and the Alamo — we lost.

AH: Why is that?

RW: I think because Americans are very uncomfortable with the idea of conquest. Our picture of ourselves is much closer to Turner's — we are a peaceful people, we are a people who don't fight, who don't look for conquest like European nations. At the same time, if we're pushed to a fight, we'll fight bitterly and win — but we have to be pushed. That's why Americans cite Custer and the Alamo — they explain why we had to fight. We were the ones attacked, we were the ones slaughtered. In effect, the conquest is justified by defeats.

This version of American history — of European migrants attacked on the East Coast and defending themselves all the way to the West Coast until they found themselves owning the whole country — this is the way that we picture it.

AH: Can we talk about the myth of the American West? The artists, the writers, the journalists who went West and came back without a great deal of knowledge, or didn't go there at all — were they creating something that didn't exist?

RW: It's much more complicated than that. One of the things that

48

we have to stop doing with the West is saying things like, "Here's the real West, and here's the mythic West." The two are so intertwined that there is no clear boundary between the real West and the mythic West. One of the ways you can see this is to read some of the diaries about going across the plains. The original diaries mention very few contacts with Indians. No violence. Where they do discuss contact with Indians, the Indians were either exchanging goods or helping them ford rivers or something like that. In their old age, when the diarists write their memoirs, working from diaries that are literally right in front of them, they construct a mythic version, the version that is supposed to be, by rearranging their lives in the appropriate way.

One of the best stories in this vein is about Kit Carson, in which Kit Carson rides into a Hickory Apache camp to rescue a white woman, whose name was Mrs. White, unfortunately enough. He rides in and what does he find? Mrs. White is dead, the Hickorys have fled, but he finds a book about Kit Carson, which he sits down and reads. What is the book about? It's about Kit Carson rescuing white settlers and killing thousands of Indians, both of which he has just failed to do. Well, what is his response? It's to write his autobiography, which replicates the mythic Kit Carson. So at which point do you begin distinguishing between the real Kit Carson and the mythic Kit Carson?

AH: So the American myth is that whites settled the West when Indians were there long before, and the whites justified their actions by making of the West what they wanted it to be?

RW: Well, there's also a long history of Indians shaping the Western environment. Another boundary that's often drawn in the West is that between wilderness and civilization. In the modern version of the West as wilderness — you can see this in the movie *Dances with Wolves* — the old West, the wilderness West, was the best place there ever was, and we've destroyed it. The older version of the West as wilderness is that of a wasteland that had to be conquered. The fallacy in both versions is the notion that the West was wilderness, when it wasn't. Indian peoples lived here. This was an occupied place, occupied by people who had their own cultures, their own ways of dealing with things. First the Indians, then the Spanish, the

French, the English, the Russians — all kinds of people, long before the American arrived.

AH: We have great misconceptions, then, about the Indians and our relationship to them.

RW: Yes. And it can become very complicated stuff. Take the New Age Indians, and people who have visions of Indian ancestors. Indians have become an environmental symbol, where Indian spirituality is the core of a set of beliefs for urban, middle-class America.

AH: Everybody wants to claim a sixteenth relationship.

RW: Right. Everybody has a Cherokee grandmother. And if they don't have that, well, then in another life they were Indians, or the people they feel affinity for today are Indians. What these people are doing, really, is creating Indians. There's no interest in actual, everyday Indians who live all around them. In the Puget Sound area, New Agers pay no attention to the Nisqually, Puyallup, Lumi. They're interested in Chief Seattle, who gave them his famous speech. Chief Seattle's speech is wonderful. He was a New Age Indian before there was a New Age Indian. He's spiritual. He talks about his deep connection with the land.

AH: There is conjecture about what he really did say.

RW: Well, we know what he said. What he said wasn't in that speech; it is totally fake. Seattle never gave that speech. Its genesis is relatively clear. The first versions of it show up in the late nineteenth century. The modern version of it was produced for a film done in the 1960s by the Methodist Church in Texas. What Chief Seattle is, is a construction. But that's what I mean. What we want is an Indian we construct.

We use him as we've always used Indians, not because we're interested in Indian peoples or their struggles but as a tool to criticize ourselves or to criticize parts of our society we don't like. That's the real appeal of *Dances with Wolves*. The Indians in that movie are totally constructed. There are good Indians — in this case the Lakota, peaceful environmentalists — and there are bad Indians — in this case the Pawnee, bloodthirsty killers. But it's all in our heads. We fool ourselves a lot of times if we think we are recovering an actual past, or that we even care about it. Because at the same time that this stuff is going on, there is also in the West a continuing, long-term hostility to Indian treaty rights, in which actual Indians claim actual privileges granted them through actual documents negotiated with Americans. A lot of the people who are so sympathetic to Indians in the spiritual sense are not going to be at all interested if Indians do something like win legal actions that preserve salmon on the Columbia River and cause electrical rates to rise, or cut down on the fishing that takes place on Puget Sound.

AH: But is this not good that we wish to take some of their culture, or what we hope is the truth of their culture?

RW: I tend to be fairly cynical about that. I think an awful lot of what we want to do is invent something we're comfortable with and attach an Indian name to it. Because there has been a long and tangled relationship between Indians and whites; many Indian people are willing to cooperate with things like that for their own purposes. But what passes for Indian spirituality has little to do with an interest in Indian beliefs. Rather, it's a sort of late-twentieth-century amalgam taken from all kinds of sources and put together with "Indian" attached to it.

AH: Would you talk about the many ethnic groups that make up the West — the way they create borders and boundaries?

RW: One thing that has always struck me about the West — partially because I was born in New York City and grew up on Long Island and then moved to Los Angeles — is there were all kinds of boundaries in and around New York, very sharp, ethnic boundaries, religious boundaries. Even in the suburbs of Long Island, people were very clear about who was Jewish, who was Italian, who was Irish — and those things made a great deal of difference. The question asked in the East all the time was, "Where are you from?" And "Where are you from?" could literally mean "Where were you born?" or "Where were your ancestors from?"

Those weren't Western questions. Western questions weren't about divisions between whites or the descendants of Europeans, they weren't about religion. They were about race. The divisions in the West tend to be racial — which is not to say there aren't racial divisions in other parts of the country. The South has racial divisions, clearly they exist in the North, but in the West the divisions are between whites, Hispanics, Asians, and blacks. It's more com-

plicated, because while there are four distinct groups, there are all these differences within the groups. Asian-Americans — lumped together are these incredibly disparate groups. The same thing with Chicanos and whites.

AH: Yet they are all very separate within those groups.

RW: Right, within them. But what makes it complicated is when that separateness begins to break down. I can see this in Asian-American students here at the university, with Vietnamese-Americans beginning to see what happens to Japanese-Americans as reflecting their experience, as if somehow the critical thing is that they are all Asians, even though there are huge differences between the Vietnamese and Japanese cultures. They know that among themselves, but looking outward at the larger West, the differences tend to collapse. You see the same thing in whites. People know there are differences between Italian Catholics and Eastern European Jews, but in the West, the critical thing is they're both white. And in Mexican-American society, where class, the regions people came from, and a family's time in the United States, make a great deal of difference within the community. But outside the community, they're Chicanos, they're Mexican-Americans, it's all the same.

AH: So, is that the new boundary?

RW: It's not new. It's been that way in the West for a long time. It started with "whites and everybody else" and with whites creating races. If you look at census data over a long period of time, they show Mexican-Americans as shifting back and forth from white to nonwhite. They show that Mexican-Americans were constructed. Also, there are all kinds of other people who once were not considered white and now are. Italians used to be driven out of white mining camps or denied city jobs because they were taking white men's jobs. But by the twentieth century, the Italians were white. New boundaries were drawn — and what's critical is that they were drawn around race.

AH: Is the West still creating itself? Is the West a piece of clay that is still being molded?

RW: John Finley, a colleague of mine in this department, has written a book that points out many things we see as typical of the West in the late twentieth century. We might not like them, but they're certainly typical: Disneyland, which Walt Disney purposely defined as not Coney Island; Sun City, which is defined as a place that is not the East; industrial parks, which started in Menlo Park around Stanford and were not Eastern factories.

I think the West is the place where the creative forces of American society are most apparent. And the West creates itself against an image of the East, as it always has. The East was everything people came West to escape. Westerners assigned the East to the past and assigned themselves to the future.

What's interesting about the West these days is the extent to which that is beginning to fade. There are parts of the West that are fearful of the future. Before, people who feared the future might be Indians or Chicanos, and for good reason. But now the people who fear the future the most are white Westerners who see themselves being overwhelmed by outsiders, who see their standard of living going down, who see the environment they came West to enjoy being threatened. If that persists, it represents a major cultural shift. In the West today, the boundary between present and future is something many Westerners don't want to cross. Because they don't think the experience is going to be very pleasant.

"...both CEOs and Ph.Ds insist more and more that it is no longer possible to speak in terms of the United States as some fixed, sovereign entity. The world has moved on; capital and labor are mobile; and with each passing year, national borders, not to speak of national identities, become less relevant either to consciousness or to commerce."

— "MULTICULTURALISM'S SILENT PARTNER, IT'S THE NEWLY GLOBALIZED CONSUMER ECONOMY, STUPID," BY DAVID RIEFF. *HARPER'S MAGAZINE*, AUGUST, 1993

THE RECENT ETHNOGENESIS OF "WHITE MAN"

James A. Aho

O N A WARM, sultry summer night, out of the recesses of a thick fir forest, a single file of white-robed men, women, and children eerily emerge, led by two torch bearers. Two hundred in number, all deathly still. Some wear high conical hats masking their faces and cut with round black eyeholes; most are bareheaded. Among them I notice several with whom earlier that afternoon I had easily bantered. Now their visages are grim and focused.

It was once believed that modernization would obliterate tribal, clan, and racial ties, enveloping people in ever more inclusive civil communities. It is now clear that this expectancy was overly optimistic. Modernization has shattered some primordial bonds, but it has fostered new ones to take their place. Even in America's melting pot, racism and ethnicity flourish. So much so that recent commentators have been driven to write of the United States as suffering from "ethnic pandemonium" (Patrick Moynihan), of harboring within its borders "unmeltable ethnics" (Michael Novak), or of the impending "disuniting" of the country because of ethnic strife (Arthur Schlesinger). While this is now widely acknowledged to be true for African-Americans, Hispanics, Native Americans, and Asians, less attention has been paid to the resurgence of ethnic consciousness in the "white" population.

In 1980 David Duke, a history graduate from Louisiana State University and former head of the Knights of the Ku Klux Klan, organized what he called the National Association for the Advancement of *White* People, parodying the National Association for the Advancement of *Colored* People, political spearhead in the struggle for civil rights by American blacks since 1920. The expressed goal of the NAAWP is "equal rights for whites." Having once seen itself as the dominant majority, Duke's clientele pictures itself now in the ever popular terms of victimization: "We too are 'discriminated against' and 'disadvantaged.'"

The founding of the NAAWP was followed by attempts to establish on western university campuses "white student unions" to inculcate "white consciousness." These were modeled after black student unions and Hispanic and Native American student clubs. Like their counterparts, WSUs fought to have "white ethnic studies" introduced into university curricula, to be taught by "racially sensitive" (white) professors and open exclusively to white students. They politicked for "equal treatment" for white students they claimed were harmed by "racist" affirmative action hiring programs and university quota systems (i.e., policies introduced in the 1970s to implement the Civil Rights Act of 1964).

The growing popularity along the Pacific Coast and in the Rocky Mountain region of a political-religious cult known as White Christian Identity is another sign of renewed white ethnic consciousness. I will discuss this theology below. Here it is enough to report that with moderate success, Identity churches are actively recruiting two segments of the "disadvantaged" white population: prison inmates affiliated with the Aryan Brotherhood and lower-middle-class high school dropouts.

A fourth and often overlooked expression of rejuvenated white ethnicity is discourse concerning the biblically prophesied Apocalypse and Second Coming. Although the United States has had a long tradition of millennialism, it was not until after 1971, with the appearance of Hal Lindsey's *The Late Great Planet Earth*, that it seized the imagination of the largest and most voluble parts of the white fundamentalist community. Doomsday fables allegorize, in terms that make sense to *Bible* students, of a conviction that "the world" (wherein "America" equates with White Anglo-Saxon Protestant values) is indeed coming to an end.

The responses to this news have been many: advocacy of rescinding constitutional amendments providing legal protection to people of color before it is "too late," then shipping them back to their alleged places of origin; organization of armed "Christian patriot" commando units such as the Army of Israel or the Army of the Fourth Reich, fighting what is said to be an already declared race war, this a phase of the Tribulation and still another "sign" of the Last Days; fleeing with like-minded families to self-sufficient wilderness redoubts in Idaho and southern Utah and preparing to defend them from "negro beasts who eat the flesh of men," from "sodomite homosexuals waiting in their lusts to rape," and "seed of Satan Jews sacrificing people in darkness." There has been advocacy too of outright secession from the United States and the establishment of a White Christian homeland.

During earlier periods of American nativist revival it was always "foreigners" who were to be sent packing. Now in the majority community there is a growing belief that white Christians have already been dispossessed of "their" country. To use patriot argot, America is now ruled by ZOG, "Zionist Occupation Government," and by the "Jewsmedia," a cabal of colored leaders and "new world order" bankers. This being so, the only recourse is to secede from the United States altogether and found a racially pure country.

There is, naturally, considerable debate concerning the exact location of this proposed homeland. Some groups advocate the establishment of what they call a "Golden Triangle," having for its borders a base extending from Texas to Florida with its arms meeting at the Canadian boundary. Others favor a region further west. One proposal suggests giving New York ("Hymie Town") to Jews, the remaining area east of the Mississippi River to blacks, and keeping most of the west, Mountain Free State, for "whites." Due to the presence of large numbers of Hispanics in California, Arizona, and New Mexico, spokesmen now limit their territorial designs to the five Pacific Northwest states.

FOUR CELEBRANTS STEP forward making a straight line in front of the bonfire. One wears black vestments embroidered with white, and a cardinal's miter. He will serve as high priest. Another is in a brown, open-jacketed seersucker leisure suit and white shirt; a third resembles a German *Luftwaffe* colonel, complete with jodhpurs, knee-high riding boots, officer's cap, pistol belt, and medals; the last personifies a Protestant minister with business suit and tie.

A blue-shirted usher directs the single line of sheeted specters, half to his left, half to his right. Moving now in opposite directions, each led by a torch bearer, the lines form two circles, one encompassing the other, the inner circle having a diameter of about 100 feet. They are arranged around a standing thirty-foot-tall kerosene-soaked, rag-enshrouded wooden cross. Near the base of the cross a small bonfire has been lit. Blue-shirted guards are positioned at occasional points inside the circles, some cradling rifles, others holding flags of the various Aryan nations. The first priest dips a fagot into the fire, ignites it, turns and ceremonially hands it to the concelebrant on his right; he in turn passes it to the third, and he to the high priest. The last then with flaming torch steps to the base of the cross and touches it.

AFTER 1870, WHEN Germany began to compete with Britain economically, English nationalists invented a myth that Germany and Britain had separate "blood lines." The Germans were said to be of pagan ancestry, the British (*b'rith* + *ish*, hence "covenant people") to have constituted the "ten lost tribes of Israel." Britain therefore, not Germany, had inherited "Judah's sceptre" and the right to rule the world.

Known as Anglo-Israelism, this doctrine received an enthusiastic reception by American WASPs delighted to learn that their heritage as Manasseh, Ephraim's (England's) "younger brother," made them coparticipants in Pax Britannica. Immigrants to America from other countries were perfunctorily denied membership in this mythic grouping by showing through hackneyed historiographies, craniologies, and philologies that they had all come from non-Israelitish blood, and thus were not authentically "white." Some were dismissed as Mongolian (the Russians and Poles), some as Turks (the Finns), some were said to be of mixed African or Arabian ancestry (the Italians and Spanish). The Scandinavians, Germans, and Irish were proven to have pre-Israelitish heathen heritage.

In the 1940s several fundamentalist congregations along the Pacific Coast began democratizing the application of "white man," extending membership in Israel to peoples who fewer than fifty years prior had been considered alien races. They now began to be seen as one or another of the several "Aryan Nations," having allegedly come from one or another of the tribes of Israel. The Germans now were said to be of Judah, the Danes of Dan, the Finns of Issachar, the Italians of Gad, etc. These linkages were confirmed by an exotic mix of biblical prophecies, numerologies, and iconographic "footprints" that today fill the shelves of patriot bookstores. This is the legend known today as White Christian Identity.

Christian Identity congregations hold annual summer conventions at which the Israelitish "identity" of their members is ritually renewed. Two of the most important of these are Colorado's LaPorte Church of Christ Rocky Mountain Family Bible Retreat and the Church of Jesus Christ Christian Aryan World Congress in northern Idaho.

Both conventions are attended by hundreds of believers of all ages, plus undercover agents and media types. The Aryan World Congress is held on a barbwired compound overseen by a guard tower and patrolled by fully armed, camouflaged "Aryan warriors." Attendees must pass a manned guard house and identify themselves before the draw gate is lifted. The Family Bible Retreat is conducted at a mountain camp rented for that purpose. Although no guards are visibly present, entrance is carefully monitored and limited to those who have preregistered. At both celebrations there is a palpable sense of being under siege by ZOG. This lends an air of excitement to the proceedings — "Are we going to be raided?" "If so, wait 'til they see the welcome party." This helps unify the

59

congregants in their identity as a "persecuted minority."

Both the Aryan Congress and the Bible Retreat borrow ritual practices from diverse (and what would have at one time been considered abominable) sources. This reflects and engenders the ecumenical reality of Christian Identity. The body of rites include in equal parts gestures from the traditionally staid WASP worship service, the light-hearted Irish country fair, and the German beer garden (without, of course, the beer). The Rocky Mountain Bible Retreat is based on Anglo-Saxon Protestant church meeting form overlain with Celtic color (box supper meetings for youth of opposite sexes — boys bidding for the company of girls, quilting auctions, square dancing, talent nights, outdoor merchandise booths, folk games — caber tossing, tugs of war, cookie bake-offs, potato races, and the donning of Scottish clan tartans and kilts to bagpipes, etc.). Were it not for workshops on the Jewish Conspiracy, foot reflexology, and patriot defense measures, one could easily confuse the goings-on with a conventional fundamentalist vacation Bible Camp. Confusion would be less likely in the case of the Aryan World Congress. While the Congress has the same religious foundation, it gives more weight to German sentiment and hooded, jack-booted grandiosity (locating the festival in a heavily forested, gaily festooned glade, playing recorded "Aryan" national anthems, parading Aryan flags, playing Saxon games — man-of-steel contest, "chicken game" to rescue maidens, "leap of faith," children wearing Austrian aprons and head scarfs).

In either case the mix of solemnity, tension-relieving hilarity, and rowdiness, coupled with a sense of urgency, mission, and persecution, produces a shared conviction of "our identity" as an exclusive, specially chosen, superior people: the covenant nation called Israel, which is to say, the Aryans, the real "grandsons of Shem," hence the Semites, sons of Isaac (the Sac-sons).

Critical readers may protest that these linguistic associations violate convention, which sees the Israelites as a Semitic, not an Aryan, folk (i.e. the Israelites spoke a Semitic tongue, not an Indo-Aryan dialect); that the Saxons were a Gothic tribe that received its name from the Latin word *secare*, to cut; it has nothing whatever to do with the name Isaac, a loose transliteration of the Hebraic *yitzak* = laughter.

But all these denials are but the mumbo jumbo of academic

scholars, according to Identity Christians. And the proof of this, if "proof" be the correct term — for we are not speaking of experimental demonstration — is the emotional power of the Christian Identity ceremonials themselves. Who but for the most hard-hearted skeptics could deny the indubitable experience of "re-cognition," the "re-knowing" (of what had earlier been forgotten in the busy-ness of everyday life) of the bonds that link English-speaking, Christian, white-skinned and blond-haired individuals together as God's chosen people?

Ethnic groups are *objects* invented, not *things* discovered. Thus we may write of "the invention of the Negro," of "inventing the Indian," or, in the present case, of the "ethnogenesis of 'white man.'" Furthermore, ethnic groups are objects in process. This means that ethnic boundaries are dynamic and permeable; who is considered or considers himself or herself a member of a particular grouping is flexible. Since 1970, for example, the number of Americans identifying themselves in census questionnaires as "Aleut," "Eskimo," or "Indian" has increased far beyond the known birth rates of these groups; individuals with mixed ancestry frequently invoke Hispanic surnames where this is useful in affirmative action hiring programs, their "Anglo" heritage at other times; indeed what constitutes an "Anglo" is bewildering. By New Mexican standards the category includes not only English descendants, but Scandinavians, Irish, Italians, and eastern European Jews! At one time the Ku Klux Klan lynched Italians whom they considered "negroidal." Due to the efforts of David Duke, the modern, buttoned-down Klan now gratefully admits them (along with women) as "white men" in good standing.

Not only are ethnic boundaries fluid, so are ethnic characteristics. They are constantly "reinvented" by selecting elements from the common store of artifacts, styles, and images that have the capacity to highlight differences. When they no longer serve this purpose, in part because of borrowing by other groups, they are dropped for other more distinctive traits. To express their distinctiveness as a "disadvantaged majority," white activists since 1975 have parroted, with no evident sense of irony, black political means and ends. This is true for the NAAWP and its fight against "quotas," for white student unions, and for the establishment of white ethnic studies programs. It is also one probable meaning of the search for ethnic "roots" emblematic of Christian Identity. The Aryan Brotherhood and neo-Nazi skinheads unabashedly copy the formulae used by black and Hispanic prison and street gangs for identification: tattoos, uniforms, musical preferences, "racially appropriate" intoxicants, high-powered weapons.

What occasions ethnic invention is still largely unknown; once inaugurated, however, it proceeds stepwise.

First comes the identification of an aggregate of individuals as an instance of an ethnic category, say, "Aryan man." The name carves a grouping from the flux of sensory experience, excluding "them" from "us," ordering and stratifying the world.

Next comes mythic elaboration. Here the "essential" and "ineradicable" features of the ethnic group in question are delineated, showing how they are biologically grounded or rooted in ancient practices, say, in the gatherings of free, animal-skinned, blue-eyed warriors in the misty, sun-dappled meadows of Teutonic forests. Myth is crucial to ethnogenesis because it veils the actual recency of ethnic group characteristics. In this way it legitimizes the ethnic world it describes, showing how it "has to be" that way. Crucial to ethnic myth-making is the citation of "evidence" to certify claims. In the past, biblical genealogy served this purpose. In our times fanciful archeologies and genetics do the job.

Seminal to belief in the reality of ethnicity is unconsciousness. This is accomplished in the third step by embedding ethnic labels and legends in children's minds. Youngsters are not present at the originary moment of naming when ethnic boundaries are first surveyed; they do not witness the inventive labors of ethnic myth-makers and the ways they cynically mold facts to fit preconceptions. They receive the ethnic world like passive spectators, as a freestanding "natural" reality.

People rarely are convinced of the truth of ethnicity by reading stories about it. Instead ethnic narratives must be represented to them in vivid, sometimes bloody, spectacles. This is the fourth step in ethnogenesis. The dramatization of ethnic legend not only impacts the higher cognitive functions, but those at the deeper, limbic level. In this way it not only memorializes ethnic solidarity, it *fosters* it by uniting the celebrants emotionally.

The ancient Celtic cross-burning is such a rite. When presented with elements borrowed from the flag-adorned, torch-led German military parade and the Catholic sacramentary with its candles, vestments, and intricacy, it profoundly moves the participants, lending credence to their belief that they are indeed sharers of a common ethnicity: "white man."

SO IT IS at the cross-burning that the high priest in a voice resembling that of a bishop explaining to the assembled throng the meaning of a sacrament, to calm their fears at seeing something so odd, describes the meaning of what they witness. This is not, he intones, a symbol of racial violence; nor is it desecration of a Christian icon. It is instead a sign of mutuality and defense. Its source is the Celtic practice of lighting seacoast pyres as guide signals. It has, he says, become "a light to guide the white in the darkness of these times." The assembly is asked to recall vows undertaken to aid wives whose husbands languish in prison and children without fathers. Those who transgress these obligations, he warns, are to be punished by death as betrayers of the race.

An explosion of fire. Night turns into midday. Although I am standing some distance from the spectacle at the wood's edge, my face warms with the heat. I search to give my feelings words. The first that comes to mind is "power!" In terror mixed with shame at my naïveté, I realize I have for too long dismissed these people as frequenters of a harmless diversionary lark. This rite I witness goes back centuries; it connects the participants not only with each other in the present but with their faceless ancestors in the past. For a moment I understand for the first time how race is truly rejuvenated; not by books and posters, but by drama.

EPIGRAM: "Ken — Just a note to let you know your ethnic status in ISU's student information system has been changed from Native American to Caucasian." (Memo to Idaho State University student from dean of students, August 2, 1993)

MILK 'EM DRY

Larry Colton

IT WAS A dark and stormy night. Really, it was. And it's crucial to this story. The place was Lodge Grass High School on the Crow Indian reservation in southeastern Montana. The event was a football game between the Lodge Grass Indians and the Busby High Warriors of the Northern Cheyenne reservation, a game for tribal bragging rights. The Crows and the Northern Cheyenne don't much care for each other. It all goes back a couple of hundred years — disagreements over territory and boundaries. In fact, they're still fighting over land in 1993. But this story is about a boundary dispute of another kind.

This football game wasn't a battle for the state championship, or anything dramatic like that. Football teams on the reservations have never done well. An ex-football coach around these parts explained that it's because the Indians aren't tough enough for the sport, no discipline. "They're too used to being on the government dole, having everything handed to them," he said. This same coach, when I asked him to explain the extraordinary successes the Crow teams have had in winning state basketball championships, credited this phenomenon to the Tenth Cavalry. Huh? The Tenth Cavalry, also known as the Buffalo Soldiers, was a division of black soldiers sent out West following the Civil War to help settle the frontier. After General Custer got his butt waxed at Little Big Horn, which is in the middle of the Crow reservation, the Tenth Cavalry was stationed in the area for several years. According to this ex-coach, there was a lot of "tepee creeping" that went on during their stay, and "lots of

65

squaws got knocked up." And now, some 120 years later, "all these good Indian basketball players have some of that nigger blood in them, which is why they can run and jump so good." This ex-coach still teaches at Hardin High, a school on the reservation with a 50 percent Indian enrollment.

Which brings us back to that dark and stormy night. The Big Horn Valley had been buffeted by heavy rains all day long, but just before the opening kickoff, the rain stopped. The game was progressing along pretty smoothly; then in the second half, the rains picked up again, turning the field into a quagmire. That's when the problem began.

Actually, the problem started back in 1851 with the Fort Laramie Treaty. That's when the U.S. government first drew up the boundaries of the Crow reservation, reducing their land from approximately 200 million acres to 38.5 million acres. At the time, the Crows were semi-pleased with the assigned territory because the government promised to protect them from their stronger tribal enemies, the Sioux and the Cheyenne, and because it left them in possession of some of the best game country in North America, with large herds of buffalo roaming the rolling hills, as well as plentiful numbers of elk, deer, bighorn sheep, grizzly bears, fish, fowl, and beavers. Chief Rotten Belly put it this way: "Crow Country is exactly in the right place. Everything good is to be found here. There is no place like Crow Country."

Unfortunately for the Crows, the whites also thought it was a good place, coveting it for its minerals and its lush farming and grazing land. So, out went the old treaty, and in came a second Treaty of Fort Laramie. In 1868, Crow territory was reduced to 9 million acres, which was like turning Oregon into Delaware. Pretty soon the buffalo were gone, and hunters and warriors were being told they were supposed to be farmers, although they were given no training or resources to do so. Still not satisfied, the government continued to chip away at Crow land, and today, all that remains from the original 200 million acres is a mere 2.2 million. For the Crows, that's the good news. The bad news is that of this remaining 2.2 million acres, 95 percent of it is either owned or leased by whites. In other words, the Crows control only 100,000 acres of

their own reservation land. For a culture based on the relationship of its people to the earth, this land grab is tantamount to cultural genocide. The problem on the football field also had to do with diminishing boundaries — as well as the Gulf War. Because the American troops had made mincemeat of the boys from Iraq so quickly, lots of supplies that had been shipped to Desert Storm didn't get used, such as bulk cheese and powdered milk. Where did all the excess go? A lot of it was shipped to the Indians as part of the government's commodity program for the reservations. The Crows ended up with more powdered milk than they could drink. Keep that in mind. It has to do with the boundary dispute on the football field.

In Big Horn County, which includes all of the Crow reservation, the one thing that consistently pisses off the whites more than anything else is all the government assistance the Indians on the rez receive — food stamps, welfare, commodity housing, medical coverage, income tax relief, scholarship funds, lunch programs, property tax relief. "No wonder they have such high unemployment rates," bristled the ex-coach. "Why should they go to work? For most of them, it'd be a cut in pay to take a job."

Despite the freebie services, the fact remains that the government's policies over the last century have made the living conditions of reservation Indians by far the worst of any ethnic group in America. According to the government's own data, reservation-based American Indians have the worst unemployment, infant mortality, malnutrition, suicide and life-expectancy rates of any ethnically identifiable population group. In the town of Lodge Grass, the population center of the Crow reservation, the unemployment rate is 90 percent. During the winter, the pipes carrying the city's water supply freeze because they aren't buried deep enough beneath the streets, and there's no money to do the job right because over 85 percent of the bills haven't been paid. As a result, much of the town loses its water supply when it gets too cold, which is often. The town's problems seem endless: its main street has potholes the size of sea lions, with no hope for repair; a large cache of marijuana was recently seized, but no arrests were made because all but one of the town's cops had been laid off; and at Lodge Grass High, teachers

are lucky to get half the supplies they order. One supply they had to cut from the budget was the lime used to chalk the football field. Enter the excess powdered milk.

As the rain continued to fall, it began to collect in puddles on the field, turning the lines of powdered milk to liquid. Soon, it was difficult to determine where the sidelines were. Meanwhile, as the Lodge Grass Indians were driving for a touchdown, two stray dogs wandered across the field toward the end zone, unnoticed by the referees or coaches. The Busby coach called time-out, hoping to stop the Indians' momentum. When play resumed, a running play moved the ball to the one-yard line. Or was it a touchdown? It was hard to tell. The two dogs, totally oblivious to the gridiron action, had drunk the goal line.

It took a few minutes to settle the dispute to everyone's satisfaction, the referees finally ordering more powdered milk, and a replay. Now, if only it were that easy to settle all the disagreements over boundaries and borders, both physical and ideological, that serve to separate cultures. Around the Crow reservation, these barriers are everywhere. For example, in the town of Hardin, which borders the Crow reservation, the high school, despite its 50 percent Indian enrollment, does not have any certified Native American teachers (even though thirty Crows on the reservation have teaching credentials), and it does not offer any classes in Crow history, culture, or language. The French teacher explained it this way: "There's a lot of miners over in Butte who have Polish ancestry, but that doesn't mean they teach Polish in the Butte schools. Besides, it's important that these kids learn French. It'll help them in business."

68

For many of the young people on the Crow reservation, their only business will be trying to escape the cycle of hopelessness, alcoholism, and lack of self-esteem that permeates an entire people that has been set adrift in this universe. "The reservation ain't nothing but a trap," said one young man.

So how do they escape the trap? In Big Horn County, they refer to a phenomenon called the "Crow crab pot." According to this theory, every time a Crow starts to escape the negative influences of the reservation, someone in the tribe is there to try to pull him or her back down. It might be jealousy, or it might be the strong pull of the family. Whatever the reason, it's almost impossible to break out of the cycle, to climb over the barrier. There are many on the reservation, however, who argue that escaping or crossing the barrier should not be the goal, but rather the objective should be to stay put and work for change. In other words, work for sovereignty and self-determination. To hell with the melting pot.

Efforts to absorb Native Americans into the melting pot have been variously labeled, "assimilation," "urbanization," and "relocation." But to many Native American traditionalists, these are nothing more than Euroamerican terms for genocide, colonization, and subordination. They have a point. Historically, the U.S. government has systematically attempted to eliminate all vestiges of sovereignty among indigenous nations, perhaps most successfully with the General Allotment Act of 1887, which unilaterally negated Indian control over reservation land, replacing the traditional mode of collective use with the Anglo-Saxon system of individual property ownership. When in doubt, the settlers said, build a fence around it. In the words of Francis Leupp, then Commissioner of Indian Affairs, the Allotment Act was "a mighty pulverizing engine for breaking up the tribal mass."

Nothing can adequately compensate American Indians for the legacy of wars of extermination and dispossession that has been forced upon them, or for the way arbitrary borders have been drawn to pen them in. Still, an effort must be made. They must be granted the fundamental human right of self-determination.

To some, the notion of tribal sovereignty is either wishful thinking or an open invitation for all indigenous nations to secede from the country. Neither is true. It is simply an intrinsic right of a people to be free from a dominating power, and to be free to determine its own political, social, and economic destiny. What is necessary for this to happen is for the United States government to relinquish its pretensions of preeminent rights over the land, and to recognize the inherent racism of Manifest Destiny. It must be compelled to honor past treaties.

Inevitably, no nation can sustain itself without a land base, or without control over the resources upon that land. If the Indians are ever to have an economic base from which to make self-governance possible, and to get off the assistance that so pisses off the

69

whites, then these lands must be returned to native control. And sadly, that is why it is hard to be optimistic about the notion of tribal sovereignty, at least any time in the near future. It is difficult to foresee the day when the government or the white land owners will suddenly say, "Whoops, this land isn't really mine."

But the struggle must continue. One acre at a time. Perhaps it is wishful thinking to hope that some day all the economic and ideological boundaries that imprison indigenous people will be washed away like powdered milk in a rainstorm. But only then will the playing field be fair.

BORDERLAND OF CIVIL RIGHTS: WELCOME TO THE GRAND JURY

Ken Olsen

I OFTEN WONDER how I'm going to tell my family about going to jail. If it comes to that.

Will they believe I'm not guilty of a crime, even though a federal judge can imprison me for up to eighteen months? Will they believe it's worth protecting my sources, my integrity, my career? What will they say when people at church ask what their children are doing? I imagine those conservative Scandinavian-Lutheran noses wrinkling in disgust when they learn I landed behind bars for writing about the animal rights movement.

Some days, I consider never unpacking from my last move. I rationalize that if a subpoena for testimony arrives, I'll move these boxes to storage, give up my lease, take my dog to my ex-wife, and prepare for a long stay in jail. Just a few weeks ago, a federal prosecutor asked how I'd "like a free trip" to Spokane, Washington, meaning a subpoena to testify before a federal grand jury investigating the Animal Liberation Front. I declined, but I have not unpacked any more boxes.

Since I started covering the ALF two years and 200 stories ago, I've received three subpoenas — for documents — from one of the four other federal grand juries investigating the ALF. Police and federal agents call me regularly, some hinting that I will be summoned if I'm not willing to talk about my sources. These are my rewards for reporting the story thoroughly.

I'm lucky.

A Washington State University sociologist lost his freedom May 14, 1993, for refusing to testify before the Spokane grand jury. Rik Scarce, author of *Eco-Warriors: Understanding the Radical Environmental Movement*, is earning a doctorate in sociology at Washington State University. His book is about the best reference work available on radical environmental groups, including the ALF.

People summoned to these grand juries are sometimes asked if they've read Scarce's book. It contains a chapter on Rodney A. Coronado, an animal rights activist who is the key suspect in the August 1991 ALF vandalism at Washington State University as well as raids in Oregon, Michigan, and Utah. But federal investigators say they don't want to talk to Scarce about his book.

Coronado was house-sitting for Scarce at the time of the WSU raid. Investigators believe Scarce, Coronado, and two other suspects talked about the raid when Scarce, his wife, and ten-year-old son returned from their East Coast vacation a few days after the vandalism. Scarce, thirty-five, was jailed after refusing to answer three dozen questions before the grand jury. He hasn't said whether he interviewed anybody about the raid. If he did, he promised them confidentiality, necessary in his research on radical environmental movements, he says. Breaking that promise violates his ethics and ruins his chances of anyone trusting him for future research.

Scarce remains in the Spokane County Jail, five months later. Federal law allows jailing recalcitrant grand jury witnesses for up to eighteen months, or until the grand jury's term expires, to coerce them to talk. Judges hasten to tell witnesses they are not being punished as the U.S. Marshal's Service handcuffs them and leads them off to jail. The Spokane grand jury's term expires in December — if it's not extended six months. Or a new grand jury, with eighteen months to burn, could subpoena Scarce again.

Legitimate crimes are being investigated, including six ALF raids since 1991 involving five arsons and more than $1 million in damage to universities, a mink farm, and a mink food supplier. The ALF is a clandestine group that opposes animal research and has eluded U.S. law enforcement for a decade. It is believed to be organized into secret cells that don't communicate with one another to minimize damage from infiltrators and criminal prosecution. There are no membership lists, no telephone numbers in the *Yellow Pages,* nothing but the raids, occasional interviews with the press, Scarce's book, and press releases to show that the ALF exists.

Unfortunately, it becomes an excuse for the federal government to go after anyone with any contact with the animal rights movement. The government's tool — the grand jury — is to civil and constitutional rights what the Sherman tank and mustard gas were to enemy infantry in World War I.

Jonathan Paul, twenty-seven, an animal rights activist who roomed with Coronado three years ago, was jailed for five and a half months for refusing to cooperate with the Spokane grand jury. A few days after a friend, Allison Slater, visited him in jail, she was contacted by the FBI for questioning.

At this writing, Kimberly J. Trimiew, twenty-one, a target of the investigation, also is headed for jail for refusing to testify in Spokane. Her attorney unsuccessfully argued that the government should give her broader immunity from prosecution, before asking her to testify, instead of using jail to "coerce" her to talk.

Federal investigators hauled a Methodist minister and his wife before a similar federal grand jury in Michigan twice during the fall of 1992. David and Ruth Stout were threatened that their daughter, Debra, faced hard prison time if they didn't cooperate. Ruth Stout was flown to Washington for questioning by the Spokane grand jury. The Stouts believe their house was watched by the FBI. Reverend Stout's secretary was told her boss was in trouble for harboring fugitives before he had even been contacted by investigators.

Other family and friends were subpoenaed. The Stouts' daughter-in-law was offered a $35,000 reward if she could provide the right information. The net of intimidation widened. Federal agents visited the volunteer church treasurer at his regular job to pick up telephone records

agents could have obtained without ever approaching the man. No doubt they wanted the leverage of having co-workers think the worst about federal officers approaching him at work.

The government wanted to know about friends Debra brought for a visit in February 1992. Long accustomed to opening their home to everyone, these genteel folk didn't bother to learn the guests' last names. But they are under intense pressure because their daughter and her friends are suspected of being involved with the ALF. Several months after the Stouts were first investigated, a five-count indictment was unsealed against one of the guests, the same Rod Coronado who house-sat for Rik Scarce. But that only makes Coronado a suspect and doesn't convict him of the crimes.

The Stouts are only two of more than forty-five people feeling harassed and intimidated by the ALF grand juries. Former Portland, Oregon, broadcaster Andrea Austin spent months fighting a subpoena she received because she interviewed Coronado in the fall of 1991, long before he was declared a suspect.

A federal judge ordered People for the Ethical Treatment of Animals to give the names of its employees to one of the grand juries. In return, the government temporarily withdrew demands that PETA turn over a list of its volunteers. Ingrid Newkirk, co-founder of PETA and author of a book about the ALF, has been photographed and finger-printed by the same grand jury. She and partner Alex Pacheco, who has received similar grand jury treatment, are targets of the investigation.

Many of my friends automatically assume I'm safe because they believe journalists can escape most anything by invoking the First Amendment. Constitutional protection is limited for journalists and nonexistent for scholars. The Ninth U.S. Circuit Court of Appeals strongly restated that when jailed author Scarce tried to argue he has a scholar's First Amendment right — similar to a journalist's right — not to divulge confidential sources. "The reporter's right that Mr. Scarce claimed...does not exist," the judges wrote.

Scarce was hoping to capitalize on a 1972 Supreme Court opinion more liberal Eastern appeals courts have used in granting reporters a right not to testify in certain limited circumstances. He is appealing to a more conservative Supreme Court — at a time when courts around the country are starting to turn their backs on this so-called "reporter's privi-

74

lege," according to the Reporters Committee for Freedom of the Press.

GRAND JURIES WERE created in England about the twelfth century, when trial by ordeal was popular. They carried over to the United States and are provided for in the Constitution despite early indications that politics, not justice, ruled the grand jury. England abolished grand juries in 1933.

Each grand jury is a secret group of twenty-three people, drawn from voter registration lists, whose task is reviewing evidence and deciding if charges — indictments — are appropriate. They meet for eighteen months and are so secret that prosecutors can't reveal when grand juries convene, who is subpoenaed, or what the case is about. Only witnesses are allowed to talk about what happens before a federal grand jury.

The secrecy supposedly was needed to protect the King's subjects from malicious prosecution. The theory is your name isn't tainted until a grand jury decides the evidence is weighty enough for you to be tried. That isn't much of a threshold, considering the U.S. Attorney has a captive audience who hears no devil's advocate about your guilt, or a lack of evidence, before voting on an indictment. And all it takes is a simple majority to indict.

No impartial judge is present to protect a witness's constitutional rights or keep the investigation focused on criminal matters. Witnesses and targets of the investigation cannot take an attorney with them when they appear before a grand jury. They face a prosecutor and a batch of people who often get caught up in the most exciting adventure of their otherwise ordinary lives: helping J. Edgar Hoover's protégés get the bad guys. After all of this, there is much doubt justice will be served. A New York judge earned lasting recognition for declaring that any prosecutor could persuade a grand jury to "indict a ham sandwich."

The penalty for not cooperating is harsh because the penalties were drafted and refined by Congress and the courts in the 1950s, when the object was eliminating the domestic Communist threat at any price. But the litany of grand jury shame began much earlier in the United States.

The pre-Civil War South unleashed grand juries against abolitionist sympathizers and, after the South's defeat, refused to indict the murderous Ku Klux Klan. During World War I, sixty-three-year-old Eugene V. Debs was indicted by a grand jury for a speech favoring socialism and opposing the war. He was later convicted and sent to prison for ten years. Mexican leader Ricardo Flores Magon was indicted for his writings, ridiculing capitalism and opposing the use of Mexican workers in World War I. After his conviction, he went to Fort Leavenworth federal prison, where he died for lack of medical care.

During the anti-Communist era, witnesses began refusing to testify before federal grand juries on the grounds it violated their Fifth Amendment right against self-incrimination. Congress responded by giving such witnesses immunity and forcing them to testify. President Richard Nixon revived forced immunity and during three years of his reign, convened 100 grand juries in eighty-four cities that summoned more than 1,000 social activists.

Supervised by a special investigations unit in the Justice Department, grand juries went after journalists, student protesters, civil rights advocates, Vietnam veterans who opposed the war, antidraft activists, and the Catholic Left. Under Nixon's watch, Harvard scholar Samuel Popkin spent a week in jail for refusing to talk about sources for his work on the Vietnam War and the Pentagon Papers.

The secrecy is the bane of journalists like myself and scholars such as Scarce when we promise absolute confidentiality to our sources. If I'm subpoenaed to open court, where anyone can hear my testimony, it's easy to prove to my sources that I didn't turn on them. If I'm summoned to a grand jury, the only way to give my sources the same solid reassurance is to go to jail.

It's not simply a matter of giving up my sources just once. Sources are my single most valuable tool in covering secretive government and corporate bureaucracies. Confidentiality is vital because whistle blowers are usually punished. My ability and Scarce's ability to gather information turn heavily on our reputations for protecting sources. Break it with one, no matter how pressing the circumstances, and we can reasonably expect people not to trust us again.

The public, more than any journalist or scholar, is the ultimate loser. When I ask federal law enforcement officers to profile a typical member of the ALF, they refer me to Scarce's book. But this important body of knowledge will not be advanced if writers are "coerced" into submission by federal law enforcement. If we cannot research and write about controversy, how can we hope to understand and resolve it? By jailing innocent people who answer to a higher calling than capitulating to heavy-handed grand jury investigations?

There are dozens of arguments for not protecting journalists from grand jury inquisition. Chief among them is the idea that such protection inhibits criminal prosecution. That's erroneous and irrelevant. The First Amendment protects journalists because some farsighted folk decided it was dangerous for journalists to act as agents of the government. Forcing journalists and scholars to become grand jury witnesses forces them to become policemen — a rather totalitarian idea, hardly what our forefathers had in mind for the group whose charge is watchdogging the government.

The argument that grand juries protect the rights of citizens is ridiculous. The protective secrecy has hardly been extended to the Reverend Stout, whose reputation has been unfairly colored by the way law enforcement has dogged his family and church. Given the myth of grand juries, a mere subpoena, much less an indictment, often is an automatic conviction in the minds of our friends and neighbors.

Secrecy protects only the federal government from the checks and balances of public oversight. Government in secret is the most abusive and has brought us our worst nightmares — FBI harassment of the civil rights movement, the Bay of Pigs debacle, Watergate, the Iran-Contra affair, the legendary blackmail of a wide array of people by former FBI Director J. Edgar Hoover.

Allowing grand juries to continue endorses a government that can harass, at will, social activists it dislikes and writers who chronicle social movements. In the case of the animal rights movement, a powerful biomedical lobby sees its profitability threatened by too much probing and publicity from activists and easily persuades the federal government to investigate and, it hopes, to eradicate its opposition.

But there will be other social movements, other wars to oppose, and other controversial activists. As long as there are grand juries, we will be mercilessly and secretly harassed in the course of the federal government hunting a few fringe extremists.

HENK PANDER

The following drawings are from the sketchbooks of Henk Pander. The first four are from his memories of living through World War II in the Netherlands.

THE FLOOR (page 79)

There were house searches by the Germans for people active in the underground, the resistance, who were hiding Jews. Because there were few places to hide in the small row houses in our neighborhood, people crawled in the space between floor and ceiling. Soldiers would often shoot through the floors at random.

THE DUNES

My mother went to the dunes near our house in Haarlem to steal wood for fuel. She borrowed our neighbor's, the Van Erp's, beach wagon. My father was hiding at home because men under forty years of age had to work in German factories, which would surely have killed my father.

Mamma ging naar de duinen met de handkar van Van Erp en sprokkelde hout voor de kachel.

THE KILLING OF A RABBIT

Our neighbor, Mr. Schrama, raised rabbits for food. My father and Mr. Schrama tried to kill one with the backside of a hatchet. We children had to stay inside while this happened. I sneaked on the roof of the sunroom to watch. I was told a rabbit would scream as it died, the only time in its silent life.

papa en meneer schrama sloegen een
konijn dood, terwijl ik vanaf het dak van
de serre stiekem toekeek.

83

GRACE BEFORE MEAT

My father bought a rabbit for a large sum of money so we could eat some meat. Later it turned out it was a cat we consumed.

85

SEALED ROOM

During the Kuwaiti war with Iraq in 1991, people in Israel hid in sealed rooms, wearing gas masks to protect themselves against missiles armed with poison gas.

sealed Room

FAST DREAMS

Mercedes Lawry

I was in love with the marginal boys
and their slick, wild words
easing me out from familiar
to blood red dawns and thunderous moons.

Learning to taste and witness to a hunger
I had never known, we drove
down long grey streets past frozen lives.
It seemed a truer place.

There was always a desperate shadow
hovering over those days and I gave it
a dozen names, a dozen reasons.
None of it finally changed me.

Oh, those boys with slim shoulders
and quick moves. I found nothing
in their eyes and was glad of it.
This was only the beginning

of my run across borders,
flirting with any stray soul and the risk,
wishing myself beyond the pale Saturday nights
of continuous drums and dead kisses.

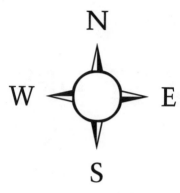

N

W ← ○ → E

S

"Men and women approach one-night stands altogether differently, the result of millions of years of sexual evolution, according to a recent study. This sexual divide hinges on the question of what men and women look for in a mate. It turns out that men leave their standards behind when scouting for a casual liaison, while women consistently maintain theirs."

—"EVOLUTIONISTS PICK UP ON ONE-NIGHT STANDS," BY BERNICE WUETHRICH. *SCIENCE NEWS*, JULY 3, 1993

WE STAND ON DELICATE BRIDGES

Hollis Giammatteo

FOR THE FIRST time in six months, I was alone. The scrubby desert outside of Albuquerque, New Mexico offered neither shade nor shelter. It was dusk. I stood with my thumb out trying to catch a ride home to Seattle. My clothes were in tatters, the color of the earth. My hair rose up from my tight-skinned, weathered forehead like tongues of flame, the tips, blond and sizzled. My bed roll and pack, loosely tied together, wobbled with every step. I had $60.

I'd been on the road for six months with five other lesbian-feminists and one "undecided," and we'd walked twenty miles a day for peace. Called, "On the Line," our group had walked from Seattle to Amarillo, Texas, Pantex, to be exact, the final assembly point of all nuclear weapons in the country. For six months we'd shaped our lives into an example of vigilant attention; the goal — to encourage those communities closest to the railroad tracks to protest the White Train as it sliced through them with its cargo of warheads.

It was going to be hard to shuffle the walk experience back into the deck of ordinary life — highway life, truck-stop life, alcohol and nicotine life, make-a-living life, pay-the-rent life, and life back in Seattle. We had walked 2,700 miles, holding our attention on the

Train in the fragile hope for a safe world. We wanted a world where people trusted and respected each other. Could we sustain this among ourselves? No. Enthusiastic but naïve about group dynamics, we'd lacked even the foresight to build conflict resolution skills among ourselves. Exhaustion over the months eroded good will and always contested our faith in the action. The pain of the gap between the good cause, with its emphasis on our spiritual values, and our brittle selves, glad finally to be disbanding, made me want to sit quietly somewhere and reflect. I knew getting home would also be a journey. I didn't want to clap my hands, click my heels, and be done. So in the spirit of the walk, at least that part that had turned me into a pilgrim, I hitchhiked to Christ in the Desert, a Benedictine monastery outside of Abiquiqu, New Mexico. For a week, I had risen and chanted the Psalms with the brothers, eaten their fragrant, wholesome food, worked in the garden, until the October storms began to rumble down the canyons bringing sure signs of fall, and it was time to leave.

Still no ride. I was worried. There were 676 miles of lava beds, reservations — military and Indian — mountains, mesas, buttes, dry lakes, and deserts between Albuquerque and Barstow, California, where civilization more or less resumed. I pulled my thumb back in, figuring to walk all night if need be, which was precisely when Bob came skidding to a halt.

He was kicking the tires when I caught up, and barely looking at me asked, "Ever ride in one of these?" It sounded like a dare. The cab was classy, a metallic-flecked burnt Sienna with lighter pin stripes like flames across the sides.

"Lots," I lied.

He flicked his cigarette into the highway. "I'm going as far as Sacramento," he said

Scared of the deserts, I wanted to make it as far as Flagstaff that night, 400 miles away. "I'll go at least as far as Flagstaff, thanks," I said. My fear had decided me quickly. In spite of his studied meanness, bad teeth, and greasy hair, I climbed hand over hand up into the shiny cab.

"Name's Bob," he said, offering me a Winston. "They call me Bob the Drifter." The truck shuddered and thumped as he wrestled it into gear. He was maybe fifty. A cardboard, cut-out naked lady dangled from the mirror. "This here's a Peterbuilt. Best in the world," he shouted, dragging up a broken cowboy hat from around his feet and slamming it down on his forehead. "Now where did you say you were coming from?" he yelled. "A monastery," I yelled back, pretty sure that saying that would protect me. He'd think I was either a lunatic or nun.

"Isn't that where them Catholic monks go?"

"It's for anyone who wants to go off in the desert and pray," I said. "I needed a rest. I just finished walking across the country."

"You what?" he said. That did it. He didn't know *what* got in his cab. I flipped his cardboard nude off the mirror. "Since I'm going to be a guest here for a while, do you mind?" I asked.

"No, please, go ahead," he faltered, and waved his arm as if the naked lady were smoke hanging in the air.

The traffic lightened. I tapped my foot to the tape of the banjo music that Bob put on. It gave a sweetness to the distance we were making. America was flashing by at 60 MPH. We chased the sunset, cruising in its wake. It cast long shadows over the undulating, beige land. My relationship to the land was shifting. Six months of twenty miles a day, nine hours of daily walking, would take three days, or thirty hours of driving to undo. I sat in that thought, longing for something to help me take it in — two shots of Glenfiddich in a lead crystal glass would have done nicely.

"You see the most amazing things from up here," Bob poked me. I nodded, thinking he'd mellowed with the luminous desolation of the land and the sun pouring its blood all over. But no. He was leering down at a woman in a tiny car. Pale thighs protruded from a miniskirt, and a clean, white cylinder of cigarette bounced lightly between her fingers. He laughed as if he'd caught her doing something vile.

THE TRUCK STOP was full of men. Bob squared his thin shoulders underneath a pale green and ochre shirt. He was sliding shiny, brown food back and forth on his plate. His skin was the color of many such brown meals, laboriously digested after sitting and bouncing and cursing and smoking day after day after day. I invaded the puffy skin of an overdone baked potato with surgical precision.

He watched me. I thought of food as art. Even this scant treat was entitled to its moment.

I bought a pack of Camels. It was 300 more miles to Flagstaff. It would be after midnight when we got there. His loading was scheduled for 6 AM. There was nothing odd about that. A trucker drives for fifteen hours with a few stops for food and gas and coffee, and then arrives late in a city he doesn't know in search of a truck stop he's only heard of, to crash there for four hours, and then get up to keep his appointment at the docks and begin another day.

It was raining softly. I put some Country and Western on. We listened to Barbara Mandrell and her gender sorrow.

"Bob," I said, "I'd like to accompany you all the way to San Francisco if you'll have me." I imagined him then as an angel, leading me through the myriad dread deserts.

"I would very much appreciate the company," he said gladly, with a courtly air.

THERE WAS A double bed, unmade, behind a curtain separating the cab up front from the interior sleeping place. It was dark and airless, a den, really, smelling like newspaper and oily rags. Between the bed and the cab was a thin walkway about my length, and I knelt down in it and unrolled my sleeping bag. Dirty clothes and loose pages from *The National Enquirer* filled the narrow space. "Here, let me take all that garbage," he said, raking it with his heels toward a doorless closet. "Is that where you're going to sleep?" The question was neither mocking nor provocative. It mirrored what I was thinking — that we really hadn't thought it out.

"Hey, use the bed, I mean it," he said. "I'll sleep up front in the cab."

"God, no. I can't kick you out of your bed," I said. Chivalry tended to exact a price, I knew. "The floor's fine. I have a pad. I'm used to it. Honest."

I inflated it quickly. He took off his boots and I took off my running shoes. Neither of us took off any more. "Well, good night," he said and cleared his throat.

"Good night," I said and a pause thudded down between us like

a crow on a road, and I knew that part of him was waiting. I heard him blink a couple of times. "Come on, now," he said, "you aren't comfortable down there. I won't hurt you if you come on up with me."

"I *am* comfortable," I said slowly to the darkness. It was thick, as if the crow encircled me with her ragged wings. I was less scared than revolted. His yellow teeth and oily hair; his color, the consequence of bad food and too much smoking. There was something catching about his loneliness and pain, as if despair were viral. "And let me tell you something else," I said, rallying. "I hate talking dirty. I hate jokes and I hate come-ons, so forget it."

"OK, OK," I sensed him waving his arm again, the way he did when I pulled down the naked lady. "We're friends. I won't force myself on you," he said warmly, as if doing me a favor.

"Good night, Bob," I said with what warmth I could muster.

OVER BREAKFAST HE read his *National Enquirer*. I read *Newsweek*, and had a pot of herbal tea. I looked out on the parking lot where bluish exhaust hovered like a toxic cloud. Some morning freshness brought an image of the monastery back to me, of the brothers filing into their adobe chapel at six, cowled, their black robes swishing. I remembered the brush of their footsteps against the hard, dirt floor. It was cold that early, and I sat on a low wooden stool wrapped in a coarse blanket, anonymous and unsexed. Brother Dan would light the candles. Our shapes would take on weight and color then. We'd been wafer thin in the darkness. Then they'd chant the Psalms, their sweet tenor voices offered to the rising sun and the canyon, and the rock and the dawn would pour through the huge, paned windows. In the two naves, the beautiful, roughly carved virgins waited to have their candles lit. I sighed, and picked up the tab. We had agreed to take turns paying.

City driving in the Peterbuilt was different from the highway, like steering the S.S. United States through the tiny colonial streets of Philadelphia. Stopping and starting and braking and turning did not bring out Bob's best.

At the warehouse, the truck got loaded with pork chops, patties, and sausages as Bob waved fistfuls of paper at the foreman's back. The inventory seemed a complicated business, broken down into destination batches — L.A., San Francisco, Sacramento — and then loaded up on palettes and stacked. "I hate hauling fucking meat," he said. "If the refrigerator unit breaks down, the whole load rots, and guess who the fuck has to pay?"

"What's eating you?" I said.

"It's just load jitters. I could use more coffee," he said. "Sons of bitches make it hard to do your job. So, what are you, Italian?" he asked, calming down.

"Yes."

"Guess what I am," he said. "If I tell you my last name, you'll know. So I won't. God, I love this music." It was the banjo tape again.

"You're Polish," I said. "You told me that last night."

There was a wonderful freshness to the morning in spite of the cracked, dry land. It would be agony to sit in this tank for the next thirty-six hours, all vibrating sheets of metal and blinking lights, in a buttocks-crushing lethargy as the fresh air and the wide skies passed by outside, unsampled. "Who wants to work for sons of bitches, taking orders and licking ass?" he sang out. "Not me. I've got my rig and me for boss. I'm free. I can travel around. That's what I like. I call myself The Drifter."

"Is that Polish?" I said.

"Another thing is, I keep my own hours, punch my own clock. A lot of husbands and wives are in it together." He looked at me as if I ought to think it through.

"I'm not interested," I said quickly.

"A man gets lonely."

"But it's a great life, right?" I shot back.

"The best," he said. He didn't see the gap between that and the message of his favorite trucker music, melancholic basses singing about the lonely miles, the painful memories, the endless rain, and the soul's real longing, which was to settle down.

"What's your favorite city?" I asked. "You must have dynamite vacations."

He laughed, lighting a cigarette, getting ready to remember.

"Yeah, I like them all."

"San Francisco?" I asked.

"Nah," he growled. "City of fruits and nuts is what I call that."

"It's a pretty town, Bob, in spite of *that*," I snapped defensively.

"To be honest, I don't see much of the towns I deliver to," he said. "The warehouses are in the bad parts, and that's what I know of the cities." He shrugged. "I'd like to know them better."

"What about vacations? You're free," I said, trying not to goad.

"A couple of days between loads. I get a motel room and sleep. Two days, blinds down. Then I have to find something to haul. I have to keep this rig moving. It's my bread. Sometimes I'm lucky just to break even."

"That doesn't sound like a great life to me," I said.

"Eh, everything's hell. I just need something that keeps assholes off my back," he said.

"Hey, Bob, have you ever been to a museum?" I said, on a happy wave of the realization that I was almost home.

"No. I always wanted to."

"Well, if we have time in San Francisco, let's go to one," I said, and sunk into a reverie, imagining us in from the desert and the truck stops, he in that dreadful hat, I in patched pants and ragged hair, standing open-faced before a lit exhibit on the tiny, delicate bridge of art.

THE L.A. WAREHOUSE was enormous, a New York Public Library of meat. The stacks towered to the ceiling, a city block of them thirty feet high. Bob checked in with the foreman, backed into the dock, and prepared to unload. Men wore quilted jackets. Lots of steaming coffee went by, lots of hand trucks, lots of inventory sheets. The air puffed and whitened around light bulbs hanging, caged, in a concrete ceiling far away. I was cold.

A fork lift advanced on the palettes of sausages and chops. Each palette had to be broken down into marked lots. Each cut was marked on the boxes in coded numbers. A thick plastic skirt separated the meat warehouse from an even larger one, where dry goods were stored. The California air came in off the loading platforms,

welcoming quaffs of humidity and salt. The foreman's quilted coat was opened now. It had to be disconcerting to pass back and forth all day from the tropics to Antarctica.

"It is," he smiled. "I get more than my share of colds." He handed me an enormous pair of gloves. Bob hadn't put a thing on over his pale nylon shirt. He seemed oblivious to the cold, a little boy whose lips turn blue from staying in the water, or a man who hasn't learned to treat his needs with reverence.

"Your friend, there, does he know what he's doing?" the foreman asked. I put on the gloves and parted the plastic. Bob was looking in the direction of his disassembled load, baffled.

"Is there a problem?" I asked.

"Well, according to this invoice, I have twelve more boxes of pork chops than they ordered," he said. "Don't tell nobody."

"Tell me where this stuff goes and I'll help unload it," I said. Bob was overwhelmed in the face of three dimensional arithmetic, which made getting home again seem far away. I grabbed a hand truck and started hauling. Bob was sure he'd been screwed somewhere; he was certain that dozen was extra. We loaded it back on; retrieved his palettes, stacked them, and were done.

As the final paper work was checked, I explored the other warehouse. Big cans and 100-pound sacks fanned out around the bottom of a floor to ceiling shelf. Rice streamed from the torn sacks. Looking closely I saw shelves and shelves of damaged dry goods. It was a bargain hunter's paradise, a welfare mother's dream, a food bank's answered prayer.

96

"What happens to all that extra stuff?" I asked the foreman.

"It gets thrown into the ocean," he said. I thought he must be kidding, and asked again. He looked at me kindly and repeated it. "I know," he said, "it is a crime. The California laws make it illegal to give stuff away that's even slightly damaged."

I turned away, sickened by the waste.

It took hours to get out of L.A. We rose at a crawl out of the gritty yellow air, up a fat ribbon of curving highway. We inched past thick, buzzing power lines and large pale houses in rich settings in the distance. The colors of the rich were green and aqua — the green of landscaped grounds; the blue of swimming pools. This was in contrast to the dominant ochre and the stinking, machine heat of the traffic coiling from the city on a Friday afternoon.

Bob had kept a pulse of cursing going, but he let out a hoot. "You know, we made some money back there," he crowed. "Dumb sons of bitches."

"What do you mean? Who's dumb?" I asked.

"Those dumb sons of bitches that loaded me up way back in Rapid City. They threw in an extra dozen packages for L.A. A whole dozen that L.A. didn't show on their order sheet." He lit a cigarette, adding the sharp, stifling tobacco smolder to the dead air.

"How can you breathe?" I said.

"I'll share it with you," and he smiled from the heart. "I mean, it's not like we're rich, don't get excited. But I bet I can get somewhere around $100 for that meat." "How does that work?" I asked.

"Easy. We stop at a restaurant and offer them the stuff at a really good price. It happens all the time, truckers selling a little on the side. No one asks questions."

It was pleasing to have acquired an extra $50. It would pad my way a little. But I didn't believe that the big ballet of America's organized abundance would have screwed up like that. I thanked Bob sincerely and waited to see what it would bring.

ALMOST IN SAN FRANCISCO were we'd part, I realized I had no plan. I needed one before saying good-bye. We were in a restaurant by the highway, and I didn't want to linger with him in my uncertainty. I was in a phone booth, dialing numbers of friends of friends and beginning to panic. He was leaning on me to go all the way to Sacramento. On the tenth ring, I hung up the phone.

It's a cinch," he said when I returned. He'd told the waitress, who said she'd tell the cook about the meat. "People are so dumb and greedy, they won't pass up a deal on meat if the shit was rotten."

"Hey," I interrupted. "Take it easy. If they're going to do us the favor of buying it, at least be grateful. You could be nice. The world is not a toilet."

His look softened. "You're right," he said. The waitress came back with my salad, a plate of brown-rimmed lettuce bits with Pepto-

Bismol colored dressing. "Cook says he'll take the meat for $80.00," she reported.

Bob didn't look pleased, but he was not a bargainer. "OK," he said, "I'll go out and get it. That'll be cash, no check."

"Would you like something to drink, hon?" the waitress asked me. I was tempted. I would have liked to celebrate getting this far in the journey. Drunk would be a pleasant place to be. Instead, I ordered Bob a salad. "Your color's bad," I'd told him, "fewer cigarettes, more greens."

Our dinners came, mine, a mound of white rice inside a ring of vivid peas; his, Swiss steak and mashed potatoes.

"What are you going to do when you get to San Francisco?" he asked.

"Stay with friends. They're expecting me," I lied. "And then move on up the coast as fast as I can. I haven't been home for six months, Bob, remember?"

"We make a good team," he said.

"I've got plans," I said. "They include getting home."

He gazed into his coffee. "It's just I haven't ever talked to anybody like this. This has been a good time for me. Haven't we had a good time?" he said.

I nodded. I wanted to say I knew he never talked to anyone like this. From the safer distance of tomorrow, I wanted to say I'd loved it too, and, in my way, would miss him. He'd given me safety, after all. But I said, because the understandings of my heart are limited, and because he was a lonely man and I was a traveling woman, "I'll see you through San Francisco. I'll help you unload tomorrow. You paid me and I'd better earn my keep."

We left it at that, finished our coffee, and went.

IN THE MORNING it poured and the storm followed us to San Francisco. The warehouse was smaller than L.A.'s. Narrow chutes sloped down to the loading dock. A cyclone fence bordered the lot, and the space left in which to maneuver was slim. The heavy rain made it impossible to see. Bob backed up, misjudged the ramp, pulled forward, stopping too abruptly by the fence. Smaller trucks

98

eased into their respective chutes. Bob turned the wheel viciously, bouncing up and down, every cell in his body charged with hatred for the job, the men who set him up to do it, the rain, pork chops, and all of California. He rolled down his window to see better and got soaked on one side, rain streaming down his hair, glasses, and face. After several more attempts at backing down, and moving up to reposition, his language built to such a pitch of violence that the air cracked, and I had to leave.

The warehouse was a long concrete bunker with a bleak coffee room at one end. I'd gotten soaked in the short time it took to walk from the truck to the warehouse. There was a pot on the burner. I sat at a table and let the coffee warm me, and began a list of my reentry tasks. Bob, still struggling, was locked inside his fury in the truck. The windshield was steamed, his face was streaming. I could see his teeth from fifty yards, and when a particular maneuver failed him, he popped up in the seat, threw his arms out, and sat for a while in his stew, panting.

The foreman came up to me. He was tall, well groomed; probably he had a therapist; probably he was gay. I couldn't imagine Bob's mood improving.

"Is that your husband?" he asked. His name was Alex.

I looked at him. "Oh my, no," I said.

"He seems to be having quite a bit of trouble," he said.

On my third cup of coffee, I saw Bob stagger toward me. I got him coffee and paper towels. He shivered, trickles turning into puddles at his feet.

"Wipe yourself off," I said. "Drink your coffee. Are you in?"

He nodded stiffly. His emotions had utterly undone him.

"What now?" I asked. "Can we get started?"

"Ever work a fork lift?" he asked. "I have a feeling in this shit hole, you're going to have to."

When we got out on the floor, things improved. His ordeal had become, in his mind, a challenge. He claimed a forklift. "Practice," he said, and showed me forward and reverse. "I'll go get my papers."

I didn't understand why nobody stopped me. The forklift reminded me of bumper cars and tilt-a-whirls, and in jerks I swung around, mastering stop and go as others glided by with shrewd competence. "I'm learning a skill, I'm learning a skill," I sang to myself with the feverish excitement of one for whom education has never led to meaningful employment. I wondered if my post-walk labors might open up a whole new set of career possibilities.

I purred up the ramp into the chilled interior of the truck, raising the fork to slide it into the central spaces of the palette. I backed out with a load towering above my head and all the way into my corner. Next load, I figured, I'd work up the nerve to turn around. Alec told me how to lay the boxes out, and resumed his paper work with Bob, checking the quantities on the palette with the invoice. I thought we'd be out in an hour.

The palettes were unloaded. I was standing by them in deep appreciation of my work, when I heard the familiar cursing.

"God damn," I heard, "call L.A.! Call North Dakota! Those bastards probably unloaded it with their order and sold the fucking lot."

"If they have it, they will have noted it, and put it aside. It'll show in their books." Alec's voice was strained.

"Well, God damn if I'm going to pay for someone else's mistake."

"Call L.A.," Alec said patiently. "Here's the number."

He headed for a phone and what happened hit me. The "extra" meat was intended for San Francisco, but had been packed in with the L.A. palettes. Bob had misread the inventory, or hadn't read far enough. So now he had to account for $100 of missing meat. I went up to Alec. "What now?" I asked.

"That guy's not all here. Now part of his load has mysteriously disappeared. Do you know anything about it?"

"Well, he was confused in L.A., and needed the foreman there to walk him through his papers, like you." I shrugged. "What'll happen?"

"If it is in L.A., they'll send it up. If it's not, he's got some explaining."

Rock music echoed through the warehouse. I went back to my corner and did some push-ups and stretched to the music as the fork lifts whirled by.

"What's that you're doing there, modern dance?" Bob asked, returning.

"It's a work out," I said. "You've been gone two hours."

"Crazy WOP," he said, spinning me.

"Oh yeah?" I said. "Dumb Polak," and we linked arms and did two doe-see-doe's.

"I'm starving," I said.

"There's machines over there that sell bologna sandwiches."

"Yuck," I said. "I'll wait. Let's get something in the city. By the way, what happened?"

He pinched his face and pulled his nose sideways. "Well, that inventory was real fucked up. The meat should have come here but it was packed on the L.A. palettes. So, I've got to convince L.A. that they've got it and then convince Rapid City that L.A. fucked up."

The lie had gotten cumbersome, not worth the $80 to protect it. Everyone was bound to see through it. On some level, though, he believed his innocence, he had that much hatred for the system, that much conviction in its being out to get him.

"Would you like the money back?" I asked, wanting to give him that, if it would help.

"Hell, no," he said. "You earned it."

W —◇— E

THE RAIN WAS pouring off him. "You're not dressed for this," I said. We'd driven the grim blocks around the Berkeley Bridge in search of a place for lunch. It looked like the flats of Cleveland, gray and industrial with scuttling people and debris. He'd parked the truck. It took up half the block, and it had taken half an hour to find the space to park it.

I spotted a health food deli, its clean windows, hanging plants and natural wood tables in bright contrast to the neighborhood. Bob blinked at the overhead menu, confused at entries like sprouts and avocado, Perrier and lime. He ordered coffee and a meat ball sandwich.

"Now, what is all that?" he said, poking my sprouts. I smiled. In another twenty minutes I'd be gone, and my eagerness was showing. "Hey, Bob, I'm sorry we won't get to the museum. It would've been fun. But the weather, huh?" I added lamely.

"Oh yeah," he said. He'd probably forgotten. "Another time." His look brightened. "Maybe Seattle. I get up there."

Then we were standing by his truck, and I had pulled my packs out. I left the Camels on the dash, and restored the naked lady.

"Take care of yourself," I said. He looked awful, wringing wet and yellow.

"This has been a good time for me," he said.

"Me, too. I was worried about getting across all those deserts. Thanks for helping me out," I said. We said other things that were the same, and didn't know how to end it. I gave him my hand. Formally, we embraced and said good-bye for the last time.

"If you need anyone to talk things out with, you just call The Drifter. Sometimes life gets pretty hard, and we all need friends."

"Thanks, Bob," I said, touched by the image of Bob's counsel in my *normal* life, my lesbian, sometimes literary, cracked, and holy life. I was touched that he couldn't reverse the proposition to say, "*I* would like to call. Someday, *I* might need to."

OPENINGS

Mary Misel

There have been many occasions to celebrate

Doors that have long since been opened

Left beckoning others.

Some doors were painted on,

Never intended to open

Taught to run my fingers along the crack

Taught to test and doubt

Manners handed out with knocking

Welcome mats rotted away in the weather

Thresholds difficult to maneuver

Standing on the inside

Looking through the peephole

At you following.

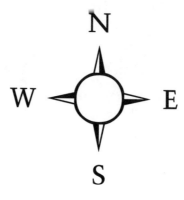

"You know what they say about para-digms. Shift happens."

— ALLAIN ROSSMAN, PRESIDENT OF EO, SPEAKING
AT THE 1993 PC FORUM

THE CURSE

Christi Killien

HER ROOM WAS the last one on the left, just before the locked doors into the Alzheimer's Wing. I looked into the room, past the empty second bed, to the window and out at the crystal blue Montana summer sky. The partitioning curtain was drawn, and all I could see was her left foot, the size seven double-A she was so proud of. It extended to the end of the bed, silhouetted in the brightness. Two years earlier, she had fought the amputation of her right foot when gangrene set in. Twenty years earlier, she'd have been out picking chokecherries for syrup, I thought. She'd be chewing pine pitch from a nearby tree while she did it, too. I knocked on the doorjamb and said, "Grandma?"

"She can't hear you," Aunt Enid said. She stood beside me in the doorway.

Enid walked in and I followed, carrying one daughter and holding the hand of the other. I was shocked at the sight of Grandma Dorothy. Emaciated, shaking, she was tethered to a hissing oxygen tank.

"Come in! Come in, Sillies!" Grandma said weakly, beckoning to us. "Oh, please let me hold that baby!"

I hadn't seen Grandma Dorothy in three years. Nevertheless, something clicked and made me act as if nothing could ever hurt me. I strode to her bedside, invincible, completely self-sufficient, like Dad had always acted around her.

"Hi, Grandma," I said. Her blue eyes brimmed. Her tangerine-lipsticked lips quivered. I set Annie Rose on the edge of the bed

near her, then flicked my eyes away, to the window ledge. "Beautiful flowers," I said.

Grandma didn't answer. She still couldn't hear me. Grandma was very hard of hearing, and she had sworn that they'd never get those damned-fool hearing aids in her ears, by damned. The reason was a combination of vanity and stubbornness and an almost pathologic need to be free of encumbrances.

"I don't wear underwear," she even announced once in mixed company. She was at least seventy at the time. Her panty hose, she elaborated, complete with its cotton crotch, provided all the undergarment she required. Grandma had to carefully work her femininity in around lots of written and unwritten precepts. She had a Dutch Reform and Presbyterian upbringing, after all, where practicality is good and sexuality is, at best, questionable.

I stood beside the bed and hugged my other daughter, Molly, to my side. Molly was almost four, and tall for her age. She stood quietly, her big blue eyes watching. Grandma was enjoying Annie Rose, but I knew she couldn't take the weight of the baby much longer. Besides, Annie was starting to squirm.

"Please take her back," Grandma finally said, and I scooped Annie Rose up. "She's beautiful."

"Thank you."

"You-you-you-you're all beautiful," she said, her old stutter returning.

"So are you, Grandma. It's good to see you."

Then she started to really cry, and Molly hid behind me. Aunt Enid stroked Grandma's withered cheek, and a look was exchanged. Enid nodded. "She's tired," Enid said to me. "We'd best be going now."

That was the entire visit.

Being close to my grandmother was always tough. I never told her of my difficulties with religion and my father, and she never told me her secrets. She'd made it clear to all of us, especially in the last years of her life, that though she loved us, cards and pictures and phone calls and visits were not wanted nor appreciated. In fact, when my father was on his deathbed with cancer, she couldn't even bring herself to talk to him.

A year or so after her death, one of my cousins mentioned her, and I had to think whether she was dead or not. I realized then I hadn't been grieving. Now, five years after her death, I've learned a story she told Enid just before she died. I believe she never would have told it to me.

Grandma had a sister we knew nothing about. Her name was Mildred. They were only fifteen months apart and grew up together on the banks of the Bitterroot River. They were very close. Enid sent me a picture she'd found of them, two young girls in long white pinafores, their hair tied up in braids. On the back it says, "July 4, 1913, the Presbyterian minister's daughters." Grandma Dorothy was ten.

Mildred got pregnant when she was fifteen, and she married her high school sweetheart. Her father said this to the young couple: "I would rather you were dead than to bring this shame upon the family." Mildred and her new husband moved to Anaconda, where she died from edema in the later stages of her pregnancy.

Dorothy was seventeen when Mildred died. She told Enid that she never forgave her father for his curse, and she'd never told anyone about it. Those were her words, "his curse." Dorothy must have believed all those years that Mildred's death was the fulfillment of her father's words, that death was retribution from God and her father for Mildred's sin.

It surprises me that Grandma Dorothy told Enid the story. Family history is a subject that both of my sets of Montanan grandparents stayed clear of. The memories are too hard, they say, serve no purpose, and as I've heard so often, are best forgotten. Among pioneer folk, the stories, like Mildred's, are buried in the graveyards.

But I have reason to believe we are connected. We pass things on, even if we don't know what we're passing on.

On Christmas Eve, 1977, in my parents' living room, I unconsciously put my hand on my boyfriend's thigh, closer to the crotch than the knee. I say unconsciously because that is what it was. I was as surprised as my parents when they outlined all this for me after my boyfriend and brother had gone to bed, and I had stayed in the living room at their request.

"Are you and Keith having relations?" Dad asked.

Why should I, a grown woman, lie? I thought. I was twenty-one. "Yes," I said.

"You are! Have you no shame? Has he no honor! Dad was beside himself. He paced up and down the room, his jaw twitching as his hopelessly misaligned teeth ground together.

Mom's lip curled. I got the feeling that she was more disgusted that I mentioned it than that the deed had been done.

Keith climbed the basement stairs in his pajamas. "Mr. Overturf, I can explain."

Dad glared at him. "YOU!"

"We are all adults here," Keith began. "We have a right to our own lives. I'm sure...."

"You sacrificed your *rights* as you call them when you deceived Christi's mother and me about your intentions! Don't talk to me about rights! Where's the talk of responsibility here?"

"Mr. Overturf...."

"Get married now!"

Keith refused, of course. Dad declared that he didn't know me anymore, that I had betrayed him. Eventually we all went to bed.

Christmas morning was tense, although we went through the motions of gift opening and our traditional eggs Benedict breakfast. My sister was fourteen and my younger brother ten. "They should be protected from this," Dad said. *I* should be, too, I remember thinking. Keith flew back to Texas the next day, as planned. He had a holiday job waiting. I had the rest of the week left with my family.

The night after Keith left, Dad stewed in his easy chair, then looked up at me with a sickened expression. "Knowing you, Christi, I can imagine that you *initiated* the intimacy, didn't you?"

"I didn't just lay there," I said, which embarrassed and infuriated him further. I was angry.

He went on to tell me that when he was in college, he had spent many sleepless nights before he and Mom were married. He had "paced the streets of Missoula" in his misery and longing for sexual intimacy, but he knew it was wrong before marriage.

I shook my head in horror at his Victorian attitudes. Sex for him was so loaded, such a huge, huge deal, it was scary.

Dad disowned me that Christmas Eve, but by the time I returned to college at the end of the week, he had yielded some. He would support me only for this last semester of my B.A., and only if I agreed never to see Keith again and to seek counseling from a Presbyterian minister. After that, I was cut off financially.

There was an apology from him in a letter almost a year later. It is dated October 12, 1978. "I want very much to be to you what I'm capable of being, and know I've fallen short. I pretty much forced you into a position of accepting me as confidant, and then reprimanded you after you did confide. I'm very sorry for that. Your dad is, admittedly, more of an intellect than a compassionate helper, and I'm continuing to work on that. My surprise and hurt ego (I misjudged how you were behaving) diminished my effort to be as constructively helpful as I might have been. I love you."

The word "behaving" made me roil. And who had asked him for help? I wrote back and thanked him for his letter but pointed out that I wasn't behaving for his approval.

He wanted our conflict to end as much as I did, I knew that even back then, but his righteous bellowings continued. It was like a poison inside of him, to yell and control.

In the spring of 1979, after I had broken off what was left of my relationship with Keith and moved to Seattle, I sent my parents a poem I liked entitled "I Loved You" by Claus Ogerman. I was still trying to separate emotionally from Keith, but I don't know why I involved Mom and Dad. Dad sent the poem back to me with his comments in capital letters after each stanza.

> I loved you,
> I love you still too much;
> But forget this love
> That pressed sadly against your will.
> WHICH YOU DISHONORED
>
> I loved you in silence
> Without hope, but true,
> Jealous. Afraid.
> UNRESPONSIBLE

I pray that someone
May love you again the same way.
DIFFERENTLY

Dad's comments confused and hurt me. Wasn't he glad I was emotionally separating from Keith? Was mention of romantic love to Dad like a fly buzzing around an open wound, or did he think the poem was about my love for him?

At any rate, one month after his fifty-second birthday, Dad died. The emotional rift was still there between us, but I got to tell him just before he died that I loved him. He told me he was glad.

My story only half-rhymes with Mildred's, but it is Great-Grandpa's curse. When Mildred died, Dorothy spent the rest of her life pushing away and trying to sort out sex and intimacy and religion. She rebelled. There are stories of her winning Charleston dance competitions in college, and never going to church. I can imagine her horror when Dad become religious and rigid, the incarnation of her father. How did it happen? she must have wondered.

And I, too, wonder. Does that account for the distance between Grandma and Dad? If I learn the stories from my aunt, and tell them to my children, will the curse grow even weaker?

I wish Grandma could have told her story. Instead, I really don't miss her. I just think about her a lot.

THE LAST FERRY

Jennifer Mitton

IT WAS AN odd, muffled sound: mechanical yet unsteady, like the bell and spring of an old Olivetti releasing its carriage at startling moments, or every time you struck a certain key. The sound grew louder as she approached the terminal.

Across the river the mountains had fallen behind heavy clouds, and even the nearest trees were pale, their trunks silver with disease. It was early November and mild, but the leaves had fallen and the birds were gone: there was nothing at all to flutter.

Perhaps the last scheduled ferry had been canceled; the lot was empty and the ticket booth appeared to be closed. Then she saw movement: deep in the ferry walked an erratic figure carrying a light.

Pearl had come to see a doctor, she had come through dark rain and traffic and got lost. She would ask the ferryman for directions.

When she reached the ramp he was gone, and she waited with the heater blowing against her nylons. Her windshield wipers gave the dark scene life, and she prayed in time with them: "God watch over us as we in our nightmares sob, for I in my nightmare dreamt that I did kill, that I would kill again."

Then through the gloom the ferryman appeared, moving across her vision with each sweep of her wipers. When he came into the path of her headlights she saw that he was walking quite steadily: only his flashlight waved like a drunken impulse. He was about to disappear into the darkness again when she honked.

He turned, and his flashlight found her car and fixed it. He made

111

an ambiguous sweeping gesture of invitation, then resumed his course. She started her car and drove in first gear toward his bobbing light. Before she pulled up beside him she swallowed her gum. An old reflex, even though she knew teachers chewed gum and fathers did not always provide.

He waved her into one of the lanes and shrugged to show it didn't matter which one. He smiled as if he had a toothache. Already it was impossible to tell him she wasn't trying to board the ferry. Many of the chronically sick have faith in magical coincidences.

The last one had changed Pearl's life. It was one morning in early October, and many of the people waiting at the bus loop hadn't done up their jackets. She stood outside the shelter, chewing at the inside of her mouth while she looked the people over — one had worn the same pair of jeans for days; another seemed unusually cheerful. Suddenly she saw a man her father's age, a man who had her father's pink cheeks and weathered throat. She hadn't seen him for years, but in an instant she was sick with rage. Murderous rage, and then, abruptly, the urge to kill herself.

Her bus came. Even a lecherous man, a man of a certain age and stiffness of neck needs to ride the bus, needs a job. Needs love and understanding and the company of his daughter, she told herself. She fantasized how she would carry out her suicide. Surely not with razors or with pills; and she had no gun. The urge was as ordinary as a gas gauge light coming on, a simple problem requiring immediate attention.

She had prayed. She was not religious, yet the words came from a part of her: "I have lost something God-given, something God gave me. God save me," she prayed, "my air is so thin."

SHE DID NOT kill herself but went instead to see a doctor. She spent all of October and most of November seeing doctors, and not one of them gave her drugs, but this last one did give her a referral. He wrote, "Ferry Terminal" on a pharmaceutical notepad.

It was a relief to drive far across the city with her referral: her desire to suicide, long diffused, had sprouted symptoms in her teens and twenties, and she worried she would not be able to keep her

job. Her telephone receiver had grown greasy with use. "Not next week," she told the receptionists at one nearby office and lab after another. "Today."

For this referral, the doctor had assured her, there was no need to make an appointment. She went straight from work the next day. Traffic stopped before the bridge: it was raining, perhaps there had been a stall. Why was it so often when you were stalled in the rain or hunting through a file folder for an old receipt that you felt sudden waves of blood, warmly rejected, waves no napkin could have held? How was it that so much of the tension in your adult life could come from not knowing how much blood there was?

THE FERRYMAN WAS still waving her on, and as she locked her car she saw movement ahead and walked toward it. (Chicks walk toward the first moving figure they see.) There seemed to be a line of figures in the shadows. As she walked through the damp darkness she listened to the mechanical bell, the Olivetti releasing its carriage again and again.

The figures were indeed in a lineup, some of them crouching, others stretching with their hands held high. When she grew close she saw the last one was naked, but she could see no farther than the half-dozen before him, and they too were naked. They appeared to be huddling on a narrow ramp covered with straw; beside them a conveyor belt jerked by with quiet but insistent anarchy. This was the old "Olivetti," and when the "bell" rang, the belt moved ahead.

There was something warm and familiar about the lineup, or perhaps Pearl had been feeling terribly cold. As she took her place behind the naked man, she felt a wave of steam so hot it took her breath away. Seconds after she had recovered there was another wave, and another, and finally there was nothing for it but to pull off her clothes, though she knew if the waves of steam were to stop, she would freeze.

She was a part of things, now.

THROUGH THE STEAM she heard coughing, the sorts of coughs

she had never had to fear: she thought of tuberculosis and small-pox, influenza and diphtheria, and from each one she felt a warm, threatening breath bathe her naked body. They made child's play of her own complaints of twitching muscles, insomnia, dizziness, and sudden internal pains — her surrogate-suicide symptoms.

The coughing directly ahead became irritating, and she fantasized about clean air ahead lower down, closer to the river. Then she saw the overhead pulley system was designed to lower the whole line down, on an angle, so only the front half would be submerged.

It would make sense to lower the front end first; surely it was a kind of natural law. But if the front end went down, the rear would have to be lifted still higher into the cold; should she safeguard the clothes that lay beside her, gathering dampness?

Thinking this over as she stood in line was like being in grade school, comforting and frightening, the possibility of being right and a bit wrong always with her. At last the ferryman came by, and she called out, "Sir!" and asked him how things were supposed to work. Had each person been summoned to this ferry? Why were they naked and standing in line?

"You'll move up when it's your turn," he said. And then, as if he wanted to soften it, "Usually a lot go out on the weekend."

Pearl began to smell their diseases and realized their cowering posture and nakedness were the least offensive of their symptoms. The young man ahead of her, chalk-colored, smelled of rotting meat, and the leprous woman before him of the worst urinal sprayed with heavy floral scent. Pearl could not imagine how she would last, and her clothes, she saw, were now soaked, and covered with a sort of molted fur. If only she could faint now, with disgust.

The belt beside her had been moving steadily, carrying nothing, but now plates of fresh food appeared, rolling past with each muffled ringing of the bell. Ahead she saw arms reaching out, but Pearl could not move. She studied the different foods and the man ahead of her and tried to guess which plate he would select.

She saw he was a young man — perhaps not yet twenty. Steak and fries? A many-layered sandwich? Astonished, she saw him reach for a dish of sliced cucumbers, and now the smell of vinegar marinade was strong, and all at once she was in her place at a smooth white kitchen table, eating her fifth or sixth slice, the sun coming through the window in a warm bar that did not quite touch the dish of cucumbers. The dish was Melmac, and moments earlier her mother had wiped it at the dish rack. It was bluish in color, light but solid, nothing like the sky or any other blue she could think of. Beside her was her turkey-vegetable soup, untouched, because something about it, the smells mixed together of carrots and turkey, perhaps, always made her throw up. Her teacher had been sick in the morning, and she wondered if she would be sick again in the afternoon or if she would return: with the substitute no one had been allowed to work on the Space mural, and the substitute did not know how to do Music.

She considered not breathing through her nose while she ate a spoonful of soup. It was homemade, and her mother would be hurt if she didn't eat it. But for the moment her mother's back was turned, she was wiping the cutlery, and there was something savage about the way she let each wiped utensil crash into its tray. Pearl had an inspiration. She stood with her hands holding the sides of her bowl of soup. The bathroom was open; the sunlight danced on the basin. She wouldn't use the basin: it would get plugged. She stood, suspended in her excitement, and then she heard her father's steps on the back stairs. The screen door snapped, and then he stood in the doorway, surrounded by a cloud of frozen air and sunshine.

Pearl hadn't given him a thought since he left the breakfast table, when she saw her mother tilt her face up from spooning out porridge to kiss him good-bye. Now he was breathing all over the room, infecting it. Everywhere Pearl looked, there he was, still smelling faintly of aftershave and hair tonic.

She slid back into her place.

She waited until he was seated and served. She waited until he had taken several spoonfuls, buttering slices of bread and eating them in three wide, wasteful bites.

She held her own spoon over her soup, dipped it, brought it to her lips. "May I please be excused?" she finally whispered.

But her father said, "Eat your soup, it's delicious," and his anger vibrated all the way to the middle of the night. Then Pearl knew she was causing the bloody and terrible silence of her mother's beating, that even her mother's bruises and damaged hearing were not sufficient: she knew she would have to offer herself up to her father in payment.

THIS MEMORY FADED, and the conveyor belt came back into focus. Pearl watched tantalizing art supplies go by, neat and bright in their unopened boxes. Here and there were ordinary school supplies she had used as a child, but even these looked clean and appealing: even the stacked pink erasers needed affection, asked to be chosen. Pearl pressed her lips together, and the old Olivetti went "ping" and carried them on.

THERE WAS AN interval when nothing came by. Pearl's body was coated with sweat; her scalp began to itch. By a wonderful coincidence the next items were pints of beer, a steady line of them, bubbling and cool-looking in their frosted glasses. The boy ahead took one and drank long, and Pearl needed no better advertisement: she too took a glass and drank until the rising tang of bubbles stopped her.

Immediately she felt a wave of dust. She sat on an old flight of stairs looking across at the other stairs and fire escapes on a street she had lived on in Montreal, her first big city. With her was Luc, wearing his suede-fringed jacket. Luc drank from the brown bottle and then, laughing, handed it to her. She felt her breasts under her secondhand sweater: full and almost too cold for sitting outside in May without a coat.

The snow had melted all at once, and she and her roommate dragged the rug outside. Her roommate beat it with her hands with the strength of kelp-liver vitamins and being American. Pearl banged the broom against it, awkwardly.

She felt the dirty breeze lift her bangs: damp but still blonde as a password. Not such a bad memory! But as she sat, she saw her mother take this photograph from the letter, and with small, sharp hospital scissors, cut Luc off. And she remembered herself, underneath him, waiting for him to stop his proud pumping. She had a longing, but it wasn't to bury her face in his flat brown hair, or to kiss his lips — lips that disappeared when he smiled. Then she saw her next boyfriend. Perhaps the longing was for him? Her prince.

She shut her eyes, but he continued to shuffle toward her, bent on his apology. Frantic to stop the memory, she reached to touch the coughing, naked boy ahead. His flesh was real flesh, and the instant her fingers made contact she smelled coconut and heard the roaring surf.

They lay, still naked, beside one another on the hot white sand. She saw that the boy's stomach and thighs were covered with open sores, and when she sensed he was about to roll over, turn to her, she groaned aloud. Perhaps this time she was allowed to faint, because it seemed a screen flew up instantly between them, and at her fingertips was an electronic console.

Select: Season/Weather was lit up, and instantly she relaxed into this soothing binary task. Ahead she could make out the boy's screen — he was alone now on his tropical beach — and she saw that others further ahead in the lineup were involved in different landscapes. Pearl selected *Spring, Warm and Overcast*, and for *Actors' Average Age* she chose *12-18*.

She pressed *Go* and smelled a wave of cypress-scented air. She was standing on her ten-speed on a suburban crescent, leaning over the handlebars and feeling the air on her back where her T-shirt slid up from her jeans. She watched her younger self turn to Joy Sanders. (Joy Sandwich, the boys called her, because she was thin, but there was sex in this nickname, and everyone worshipped Joy's long bones, her long black hair.)

Pearl turned up the *Volume* and heard shouting from their friend Irene Sawatsky's house. Irene was getting permission to cycle into the mall.

Then Pearl saw another control: *Identification*. She turned the dial to *Closer* and was immediately filled with a restlessness she hadn't felt for years. Now she was leaning against jewelry counters, now prowling through the lingerie and sweaters and shoes and makeup, ducking past the mentally retarded security guard and then, oddly, now she saw her boyfriend's ex-girlfriend — the one who had once declared at a dance that Pearl wasn't dressed well enough to get in.

Through all these images she worried she would not be able to keep up with Irene and Joy on the hills. Irene was fat but strong, and Joy would dare anything if Irene wanted her to.

On her own, Pearl avoided hills. It was possible to take a route all the way to Poco with no hills, but the mall was farther. You chose between the long hill the Port Moody way, or killer hills going past the asylum.

Irene and Joy had already stolen albums at the mall, and Irene had stolen a knee-length leather coat and modeled it outside the café on Friday night, her pretty lips frozen in a smile.

N W—◇—E S

PEARL FELT THE ferryman's whiskey breath before she turned from the video. He reached across her and turned down the volume. "That mall," he was saying. "Was it upscale?" He peered into the now quiet landscape he had silenced: three long-haired girls cycling toward a river, preparing to cross the bridge single file.

There was something about the ferryman that made her feel sick, the sickness burrowing through her insides and wanting to come up her throat. He turned *Identification* to *Further,* and Pearl caught her breath. "It was a suburban mall — families…kids…."

The ferryman nodded. "We didn't have malls when I was a boy," he said. He paused. "You're here to see the doctor?"

"Is there one? Yes."

"We have to run a check on you first," the ferryman said, and then, with the same grim smile, he turned *Identification* back to *Closer* and walked on, his flashlight bobbing from one landscaped screen to the next.

N W—◇—E S

PEARL HAD NEVER stolen. In stores she looked for what the popular girls were wearing, and sometimes there was the money to buy a top. Today she knew she was following Joy, whose parents had lots of money, and who stole all the time. She was going to see how it was done. But now Joy had disappeared, leaving Pearl in the Young Ingenue section with her bra hook digging into her back, the sweat from cycling having brought out her new allergy to metal.

She couldn't reach behind to adjust the flap over the hooks because the saleswoman was already watching her.

Before her were mohair sweaters, each shade filling a cubby of glass and metal tubing. The sweaters were soft-looking, like pastel hamsters. She touched a pink one, felt the saleswoman watching her, and picked it up. Then she took a cream one and the blue one and then a silver one, and a second silver one, quickly, as if such a wide range of color might obscure the facts.

They were all tight around the neck. The silver one would look good on Irene. She could see Irene's eyes turning misty violet inside her black eye-liner, her sun-bleached hair flat over one cheek. But on Pearl the sweater looked plain gray, and her eyes were as usual, no, worse than the way she was used to seeing them in the bathroom mirror. "I have never stolen," she thought. She pulled her navy sweatshirt over the gray sweater and took her time browsing through a rack of blouses before she left the store.

Joy and Irene were eating hot dogs. "But we'll wait," Irene said cheerfully, with a sparkling hint of menace. Pearl was too jumpy to know if she herself was hungry, but she bought a plain hot dog and ate it quickly, sitting with Joy and Irene on the imitation wood benches. Outside, the warm gray sky made her sleepy, and under her sweatshirt, the mohair began to itch at the back of her neck. Her legs were tight from the ride in. I will never do this again, she was thinking, but already Joy and Irene were talking about coming back the next Saturday.

Pearl remembered school a few years earlier: she got a low mark on a science quiz and so could finally enter the club where you had to have bad marks: C or C- at best. But when she inquired, the standards had changed: now you needed a D to get in.

It began to rain as she passed the mental institution, and Pearl speculated about the extra calories this would make her burn. She was far behind Joy and Irene, but they were waiting at the turn-off.

"Did you get anything? You took so long, we thought you got caught."

Pearl pulled out a bit of gray mohair fluff. "It's like wearing a cat around your neck," she said.

THE SCREEN WENT dark, and the ferryman was beside her again. "That's not why you're here," he said roughly. "You were a kid. We didn't have malls," he said again. "We sat on the porch, and if we had a nickel we bought a big bottle of Coke."

He was still talking when she heard the first meows. She loved cats and right away she was looking for kittens. A homeless mother cat might like it down here — there must be mice or rats. The ferryman turned away. On impulse she reached out, touched a bit of his orange jacket. "Let's say you belong to a group of unlovable people," she began.

But the ferryman said he had to move on. He left Pearl with her thoughts: if you belonged to a group of unlovable people, grown up now, fatter and even more unhappy than when you were sixteen, nevertheless you must not suicide, your simpering lips must keep admitting you could get your hair done at an expensive salon, or for God's sake buy some cut flowers.

She was crying by the time she understood to whom this particular voice was addressed: it was to her mother. Why did you stay with a man who did not speak for months and years except in rage, a man whose movements were random and scarcely performed? It was the voice of women writing in their journals to complain about their mothers: it was her own voice.

She managed to stop the ferryman on his way back.

"And the worst for them was they had me," she told him, "a shrinking brat: shouldn't I have hurled myself out the window?"

The ferryman looked uncomfortable. "You might have written them some nice poems," he said. He was trying to remove a speck from his eye.

"Then I must be here because of my abortion," Pearl said boldly.

The ferryman looked blank, and only with his own voice seemed to regain his stride. "Abortion became illegal only in the 19th century," he said. "Efforts to legalize abortion have increased in response to population increases, pressure from women's rights movements, and a high maternal death rate from illegal abortions. Opponents continue to press for prohibition, but no one gets sent here for having abortions." He started to go. But Pearl held him back. She needed to talk about her abortion.

"We were a couple new to our bodies' fire," she began, "our young-thorned bodies dry with thirst appearing, disappearing through the night." The ferryman looked sullen. "He always wanted toast," Pearl continued. "I would have made him a real breakfast, but he wanted me to leave so he could get to work."

The ferryman took a paperback from his pocket and, bleary-eyed, found his page.

"There was no plan for it: *abort* meant to miscarry, disappear, off, away + to arise, appear, come into being. I would not have enough to offer this baby. No father. Worse, a father who doesn't want to be a father. Who does not love the mother. And I, my little baby, I shook on my two feet, ever the unready." Pearl stared at the console, and its dark dissolved into a pork chop sizzling under a low ceiling, under a white plastic spatula melted in one corner.

There was no God for her. Nothing now was right. O Prince, are those your lips? She saw them pink and swollen. There were so many pink erotic things, and some ended in babies. Kettle on. Face washed. This baby would die: nothing now was right, not the green color they had painted the walls. Mornings were at least more practical.

It was the day after the day he took her urine in. He got positive results of course. He told her he thought all day about keeping it, but he got so scared, felt so useless. "You're so right for me and I'm all wrong for you," he said, and told her he had lain on the floor and cried. And staring at his weak face Pearl decided there was nothing to live for except other people's children after she murdered her own.

"I knew I would go mad," she wanted to tell the ferryman. But he was up ahead now, speaking with someone with more seniority.

At the time she had considered jumping on a plane for England, where she had a friend. There she'd be, in England.

She was alone and without God.

She walked into the clinic, the modern Church of Referral. She learned that her permanent would be relaxed from the anesthetic. At twenty-two, her counselor had already had two abortions, and would have another. Large canvasses of acrylic female genitalia covered the walls.

Pearl did not want to be sold a code of conduct, was not doing this for women; she just didn't have the good fortune to swell with her baby and croon. Perhaps she didn't deserve it.

"You're being pressured to keep it," said the girl. "But don't give up." She gave Pearl a referral.

Pearl found that when you are waiting for an abortion nothing happens. There is nothing to tell. She phoned nobody and wrote nothing and did not pick blackberries, no matter how many she saw. Afterward, she imagined the sheets dropped into boiling bleach, her own bloodstains thin and dull. Her thoughts returned, whistling past steel carts through the thickly painted hospital corridors. Leaving no traces no birds no singing anywhere.

"No, it was negative," she told her Catholic co-worker whose boyfriend was always offering, drunk at least, to marry her. "Probably it was stress."

What they did was bring the pregnancy to a premature or a fruitless termination. In morphology spines are aborted branches: we have morphologically sinned, you with your male breasts aborted teats, me with my empty result.

The practice of abortion was one to which few persons in antiquity attached deep feelings. Deep feelings of condemnation, failure of aim or promise, the empty result of any action: in other words our whole relationship, thought Pearl, each time she saw a baby, heard of another abortion.

The empty result was that she never tired of the empty result.

In the recovery room she cried herself out of the anesthetic. "If you are the doctor! If you can hear me! Please!" She in her nightmare learned that she had killed, would kill again. And was given orange juice in the name of the dead.

The cab driver could smell blood. He drove many women home, refusing to kill them though their despair made them beg.

Later, in her room, on her own again, then in another relationship then out again and then, and after that, the story always ends. There is nothing anyone can do.

A woman can miscarry without knowing she has conceived. Something mechanical out of control, the bell and spring of an old Olivetti releasing its carriage forever. The woman could be stirring noodles, or be stalled on a bridge, or hunting through a jammed file for some old receipt. At any time a woman may feel a rejection of blood. She must always scrub the streaks from her panties, scrub out the runes of waves no napkin could hold. Scrub and rinse until her fingers are ice and the water clears.

But you chose to miscarry! You chose to abort! Pay and pay the price! There in the lineup with the festering boy before her she prayed: "God I have miscarried something God-given, something God gave me, God save me, my air is so thin. The leaves do not flutter, the spruce does not complain. God watch over as we in our nightmares sob, as we in our nightmares learn."

The boy ahead of her stank. "These unlovely people," she told the ferryman, when he returned, "are people whose jeans have not been washed."

"They can take them off," said the ferryman, ignoring, as she had, that the entire lineup was naked.

She was still praying: "As we in our nightmares learn that we have killed and must kill again."

"You were *kids*. You were a couple of young people," the ferryman said.

"New to our bodies' fire," she agreed, nodding, surprised he remembered anything she had told him.

He was shaking his head. "It wasn't the abortion that got you here: it's the living ones you abandoned," he said.

Then she remembered the cats.

"No one comes in for abortion," the ferryman added. "It's things they've forgotten, things they didn't feel bad about."

Now she heard the meowing. It was leaving the cats. "I have been allergic to cats for years," she explained. But now she could see the cats she had left behind. After hatching, she told the ferryman, chicks go toward the first moving object they see. Did she bond with the cats, or did they bond with her? Even now when she saw a cat on the street trotting through the mush of autumn leaves she called to it; she knew them all.

The ferryman listened. "So you left them with your father. You ran away, but you left your cats with him. You knew he would get rid of them."

"I couldn't stay with my father," Pearl said.

"You didn't want to?"

Sometimes you want to tell the truth so badly you would give up pleasure: you would give up all sensation. But all around her were stinking bodies, and what was the truth if you didn't know it?

The water below was violet covered with yellow oil. She wanted to be dead. Why couldn't she stay with her father? Because her father was crazy. Why couldn't she just be allowed to die instead of remembering? Her father fooled people — even now she needed multiple opinions, could not trust her own. His effect on her. He was inside her now, out of control. If she killed him she was the one who would die. She didn't want to think. She had a headache. She despised herself and wanted to die. "We don't learn from our mistakes," she told the ferryman, her mouth turned down with disappointment. "There's no reason to stay alive."

"Most people would have done the same thing," the ferryman said. "They would have left the cats." But his objection was mild; it too was part of his job. He showed her a form requiring her signature. It was near the end of his shift. He had nothing to live for: all he did was push people over the edge. "You are given one last chance before you sign," he said. He took a manual from his pocket, found the page and read: "Please imagine you are small again. You are in the bathroom. The adult in charge is about to drown the new kittens."

Pearl could hear the mother cat meowing. The kittens, of course, sounded like mice. She saw the mother cat circling around her father's legs. She was about to right the past! Never had she felt so good. But when she grabbed the kitten from her father, she saw it was missing much of its fur, and the soft bald patches were crowded with tiny black balloons.

"Ticks," the ferryman put in, and Pearl thought she might faint. The mother cat appeared with three more infested kittens.

"Are they going to die?"

"Of course. You shouldn't touch them," he said.

"If it's poison I'll be happy," Pearl whispered. But her jaws had come together. She could not reach out; and she could not open her mouth to speak when the ferryman asked if she'd be taking the cats along home.

The ferryman left her for several hours, but by the end, she could no longer look at the cats. The boy in front of her was gone, in fact, all the people who had been ahead of her were gone. She was now at the head of the lineup, and below her was the violet water. "Please," she begged the ferryman. She said it through her teeth, because she knew now that he had always been her father. If nothing else, she prayed, let him do his job.

"Cicero warned that not to know what happened before we were born condemns us to always remain children, and in an aesthetic sense, that is the punishment to which we have condemned our own children. It is a mystery to me why our study of history revolves around wars rather than artistic accomplishments, around the writings of politicians rather than those of pets and essayists. To be locked out of sights and sounds, rhythm and meter, is as numbing and dehumanizing as to lack the ability to read."

— JOHN FROHNMAYER, IN *LEAVING TOWN ALIVE: CONFESSIONS OF AN ARTS WARRIOR*

THE NEWS

Christopher Howell

BEFORE CONFUCIUS SAID "No" it was Chinese custom to immolate living dog, servants, concubines, and wife along with the wide-eyed and carefully painted corpse of the nobleman. The Other World was thought to be far away and glittering with necessities only a peasant or a eunuch or a woman would go forth to all alone, like a fish battling great rivers on the way to death.

It was widely reported that sacrificed women wept exclusively for the dearly dead, never for that savagery death had ignited all around them. Even the dogs and horses, it was said, mooned only for the master sent alarmingly off ahead of them, and so, with the wisdom of good beasts, were anxious for the flames to scorch apart the veil dividing flesh from light and let them down, free, on the eternal paths of servitude and love.

As fire crept up the racks of fagots, chewing faster and faster like a famished menace, some claimed figures in the blaze kowtowed, smiling bodhisattvalike into their last earthly moments or clapping with expectation. Actually, Confucius tells us, they screamed, like nothing else but creatures burning in the ruins of their lives, so that no amount of mourning brought relief to those who heard them, everyone shuddering for terrible death, desperately, as today we shudder at the small starving faces brought to us in the evening as we eat. And those watchers long ago, before Confucius, said finally there is nothing we can do until a wise man comes to tell us, "This is unseemly. This is mad."

127

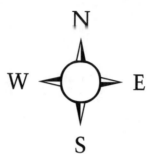

"The most potent political force shaping the civilization of the future may well be one that has no place in any ideology: the sheer movement of people from one place to another. It is changing the face of the world, rendering old boundaries and policies obsolete, and laying the foundation for a 'new world order' quite unlike anything foreseen by any political leader or theorist — a boundary-less world in which people live where they choose."

— WALTER TURETT ANDERSON, PACIFIC NEWS SERVICE, DECEMBER 7, 1992

NO SOIL REQUIRED

Robert Michael Pyle

TIME WAS WHEN we were fairly clear about the difference be
tween life and death. Always the artificial has been with us, but
without pretense. The plastic flower in the graveyard fools no one,
nor is it meant to. So it is with the lumps underneath: we may speak
of "afterlives," and some feel spirits among them, but there is no
doubt really: the people we plant, like the fake flowers that mark
the spot, are dead. We who remain, and the weeds that creep over
the graves in spite, are alive. The line has always seemed, to me, a
sharp one.

Now, as we rush to embrace death in so many ways, that once-
clean distinction is blurring. Of course there are the so-called "he-
roic measures" for supporting the life of the living dead. There is
the titanic battle to position the moment human life bestirs, at con-
ception or birth or somewhere in between. These are not new. But
now we find muddy ground as well when it comes to defining what,
indeed, constitutes an organism — a living thing. Some say viruses
are lifeless until they kill; others insist computers are alive and will
soon reproduce. Is the earth a living thing? Is an anthill an organism, like a colonial jellyfish? And what about shopping malls? I've
heard it proposed that these are the coming evolutionary units, with
consumers as cells and products as nutrients.

Actually, it was in a shopping mall that I lost my footing in the

slick and fuzzy DMZ beyond life as we knew it. Waiting for a tire change at Sears, I roamed the dreary aisles, seeking a manner of spending the afternoon that wouldn't offend the ghost of Thoreau, who said, "As if you could waste time without injuring eternity." Giving cursory inspection to a vendor's table of "Southwestern" figurines and other dross, my eye raked something that looked alive. Tucked among the song dogs and shamans, there were plants — cacti, succulents, bromeliads. They offered a moment's diversion to this fish out of water, but their removal from their habitats to this space station seemed even bleaker than my own.

Then I noticed a basket of what looked like skinny, greenish, dried-out spiders, or curly urchins. The sign read "AIR PLANTS — Tillandsias — a living plant that needs no soil. Just a little mist a couple of times a week and your love and they will grow and have babies." A suitable plant for malls, I thought — nature reduced to little parcels of weirdness, like Lava lamps and fiber-optic sculptures — trophies for jaded shoppers to take home and love, with no care required; no messy soil. Well, who was I to sneer? At least they were alive, and we can all use more life around us. But what a life, I couldn't help thinking: stuffed into an ashtray on someone's TV, or perched among the seashells atop the toilet, sharing the shower's spray.

The air plants reminded me of something else, and it picked at me until, back home, I found it in a file: a color brochure advertising "The Windswept Bonsai — a great gift idea!" The flyer pictured a little juniper rooted in a pot of gravel, atop a grand piano. "This Incredible Real Bonsai Stays Beautiful Without Water or Light," it read, "yet retains a carefree, natural look and fragrance." The trees, after being grown and sculpted in a nursery, are treated with a cell-replacement process that eliminates the need for water, light, or nutrients. In other words, they kill and pickle it. But nowhere does the brochure mention that your authentic Bonsai is not alive. It does quote Joyce Kilmer on trees ("I think that I shall never see/a poem lovely as a tree"). The Windswept Bonsai Interiorized™ by Infinitree International. It is a product of the Weyerhaeuser Company, the Tree-Growing People, creator of Incredible Real Forests. And it is dead.

Now, I've always thought that the desire to have plants around one had something to do with the need, or at least the urge, to consort with other living things. We, the living, have traditionally sought life for company: friends, neighbors, pets, houseplants, gardens, yard birds, wildlife; even zoos and aquaria present the spectacle and the comfort of life, however out of context. Surrounding ourselves with active organisms of our own and other species, it seems to me, is both a means of staving off the morbidity that awaits us all, and a way to affirm our passing citizenship in the country of the living. But if you can make a strange plant reproduce out of any context of nature whatever, then why do you need such a context at all? Apparently you don't: you can have Incredible Real Trees in your living room or boardroom that needn't even transpire. Which implies that you could have animals that don't respire. Then the mannequins and shoppers at the mall could become fully interchangeable at last.

I remember in the vestibule of the huge gymnasium at Yale, the original bulldog mascot is preserved, stuffed in a glass cabinet: "Bulldog, Bulldog, Rah Rah Rah, E-li-Yale." With the help of Weyerhaeuser, or perhaps Hormel, some future mascot could be preserved in such a way as to present a more lifelike visage than that moth-eaten relic. Rah.

HOME FROM THE mall, I sit on my front porch and try to regain the sense of a border I can believe. Here, it isn't hard. I am surrounded by the stuff of that which is living, the stiffness of that which is not. This iron trap, for example, is not alive. This poor mole, squeezed nearly in half but still soft velvet taupe, pink-tipped at both blunt ends, its massive digger's hands still pliable — it's Incredibly Real, but it is dead too. Love in the mist will not make it have babies, which is the point of its being in the trap. But the blowfly that keeps trying to land on the mole to lay its eggs is alive. Its maggots, too, will be living, for it can make babies with nothing but love and flesh.

Beside the mole is a cactus; it's out of context too, but at least in soil and surrounded by other plants; and just now, it's making a

131

wave of big rose flowers. It is undeniably alive. In this lifeless tank, feeding on brambles that are dead but were recently living, is a giant Australian leaf insect: alive, and making babies — or at least eggs, that need to be hot and misted to hatch but don't care about love. This iridescent wood-boring beetle, emerald and gold against the white pillar, the wistaria climbing the pillar from below, and the cat sleeping at the base of the pillar, are all alive. But the pillar is dead as a post.

As for me, I am alive and breathing the mist still, if not making babies. I have not been Interiorized™ yet. Nor have I been fooled. I am surrounded by life and death, and it is all as it should be: death is seldom obscene unless out of season, or masquerading as something else. It is clear to me which is which.

Still, there is the compost pile...beneath the living hornbeam trees, bounded by a roundel of dead bricks. Only here, where the mole will go, do I lose my bearings — where the slugs and the eggshells, the clippings and bacteria, the moles and the maggots, the worms and the dirt all mingle in such a maze that the gelid breath of Death itself goes hot and the stillness of the quick comes fluid and lithe. The compost heap: region of resurrection, where the living soil arises from the wreckage of what went before. That is where I lose all sense of sides.

Yes, they argue over whether the earth is alive or not. In the end, perhaps it is only earth that is both living and dead all at once, where that mortal boundary at last dissolves. In the soil — which, it seems, we shall no longer need.

BORDERS

David Suzuki

BORDERS THAT SEPARATE nations and states determine the fate of people and entire cultures. Following the partition of parts of India into East and West Pakistan in 1949, hundreds of thousands of lives were lost while millions were uprooted and forced to migrate to a different country. Lives and futures hang on the way those political boundaries are finally drawn.

When I grew up as a boy in the 1940s, the maps of the world that I learned in geography class were very different from those my children now study. Political jurisdictions are not eternal or linked to the physical realities of the Earth, they are arbitrary and ephemeral and have always moved and shifted on the winds of history.

The 1990s have been characterized by remarkable changes in the global atlas. Two Germanys have been fused into one while the Soviet Union has been fragmented into pieces that continue to shatter along ethnic and religious lines. The final outlines of the parts of what was once Yugoslavia will be drawn in blood and forever contentious. India and Pakistan continue to skirmish over border territory, Japan demands the return of islands from Russia, the United States and Canada dispute their rights along Georges Bank in the Atlantic and between Alaska and British Columbia in the Pacific. Humankind has a remarkable capacity to claim territory and expend massive resources, money, energy, and lives to maintain and protect it.

It is said that before the arrival of Europeans to North America, a squirrel could begin to jump from tree to tree on the Atlantic coast and reach the Pacific without once having to touch the ground. Today, seen from a plane flying high above Canada and the United States, there is little evidence of that once vast, diverse, and unbroken forest. Geometrically correct straight lines, circles, and rectangles signal roads, borders, farms, and cities. Everywhere across the landscape there is the imprint of one species — us.

We even extend our boundaries beyond the land that is our normal habitat. Recently I watched two spectacular films on the big screens of IMAX. The movies were ostensibly explorations of the mysteries and beauty of the last frontiers of outer space and the ocean floor. But actually, the films were a paean to the ingenuity and prowess of humankind. Human intellect and technology have extended the sphere of our reach to the ocean's depths and beyond our atmosphere.

Since the beginning of life on this planet, boundaries were imposed on all organisms by the biophysical features of their surroundings. Through the long process of mutation, genetic shuffling, and natural selection, life evolved and changed the range of their habitat. Life began in the ocean, where it spread across the globe, then crept onto land, and eventually took to the air. But all this took place on a geological time scale.

Human beings changed that. With the advantage of a large and inventive brain, we were able to modify our surroundings and extend the range of our species from tropical savannahs to steaming jungles, arid deserts, and frozen tundra. While this human social evolution accelerated the rate of change over biological evolution,  it still occurred over thousands of years. With the era of modern science and technology, we acquired the tools to change the contours of the Earth through megaprojects and even extended the frontiers of our manipulation to our own biological makeup and the very building blocks of matter. Scientific and technological optimism and hubris have led us to believe that there are no limits to human inquiry, understanding, and mastery. Through science, we believe, the curtains of ignorance are pushed back to reveal nature's deepest secrets. Here on the planet that is our home, that boundless faith has been horribly destructive and we have created immense change in a matter of years.

With our technological muscle power, we are able to bludgeon nature to conform to our own needs and borders — straightening rivers, draining swamps, clearing forests, and building fences, highways, and cities. We subdivide the planet along national, provincial, and municipal lines that seldom reflect the geological lie of the land. While traditional lands of tribal and aboriginal people often coincided with mountain ranges, foothills, watersheds, and rivers, modern territories are more likely to be based in geometry. And therein lies the cause of much of the destructiveness of our activities on the environment. Human activities are often unsustainable and, when carried out within human borders, they are dislocated from the physical realities of the Earth.

The catastrophic fire at a nuclear plant in Chernobyl was suspected within minutes by Swedish scientists who detected radioisotopes in the air. Within hours, Canadian scientists had recovered radioactive particles over the Arctic. The borders separating Ukraine from Sweden and Canada had no relevance to the flow of air. That crisis dramatically reminded us that as biological beings, humans are a part of the natural world in which our boundaries are meaningless. Air is part of a global commons. It is not constantly being generated but is recycled endlessly by all living forms that share it. The air physically connects us to all other living things through atoms and molecules that are exchanged back and forth as gases. We are not only connected to beings currently living, we obtain atoms that were once part of all organisms who lived in the past, and our exhalations will be compost for future life forms.

It is the same with water. Over 70 percent of the planet is covered with water. That water is endlessly circulating around the planet in the cycle of evaporation, condensation and rainfall. Our own flesh (depending on which authority is consulted) is between 70 and 95 percent water! Within our bodies are water molecules that have come from all the oceans of the world, from the canopy of tropical rain forests and the plains of Africa. Like air, water is indispensable and a kind of glue that connects all living things to each other and the planet.

On land, the distribution of organisms is based on *their* habitat needs, not human-imposed boundaries. Thus, it is absurd to think

that plants carefully tuck their roots in on one side of the border between provinces, or animals screech to a halt at the border between Canada and the United States. Forests, those complex communities of animals, plants, and microorganisms, distribute themselves within watersheds or along river basins, not within straight perimeters drawn for forest companies or to define private property.

Nothing illustrates the subordination of human borders to natural ones better than rivers or migratory animals. Consider the Nile River, the longest in the world. Egypt is at the end of the Nile's journey, which passes through eight other countries. The notion that the river itself can somehow be managed within each country is absurd. Yet that's what is tried. Even single watersheds are often intersected by several county or municipal lines that render "management" of that watershed impossible.

But it is migratory animals that make a mockery of our notion of resource management. Monarch butterflies that hatch in Canada west of the Rocky Mountains follow a genetically determined path across the United States to wintering grounds in Mexico before turning back. Most don't complete the round trip as many born in Texas don't return to Canada. The notion that these insects are Canadian or American or Mexican makes little biological sense. And so it is with Pacific salmon that travel around thousands of kilometers of ocean running a gauntlet of fishing fleets before returning to the rivers of their birth. And shorebirds complete some of the most spectacular commuting, some traveling from the high Canadian Arctic all the way to Tierra del Fuego and back! If these companions of ours matter to us, we need to think differently about borders and maps.

These days governments attempt to deal with the complex problems that confront us as a result of human activity. It is necessary to subdivide these bureaucracies to handle them. But the bureaucratic categories reflect *human* priorities, not Nature's. It gets us into a lot of trouble. Take the Great Lakes, the largest body of freshwater in the world. It supports some 35 million human beings, providing for fishing, recreation, transportation, and water for agriculture, industry, and domestic use as well as a receptacle for sewage and industrial effluent. But the management of the Great Lakes is not only subdivided into different bureaucracies that reflect the different uses, they are further separated along political lines. There are two different countries bordering the lakes, so we have an International Joint Commission, but as well, two provinces and eight states lie on the fringes in addition to dozens of municipalities ranging from cities such as Chicago and Toronto to small towns and villages. Bureaucratic jealousies and mistrust often fuel turf wars that preclude the management of the Great Lakes as a single giant system.

What do we need then to deal with the ecological crisis that connects all living things to each other and the geophysical world?

We have to learn to accept that as biological beings, we are as dependent on air, water, and soil through the food we eat, as are all other life forms. That means that the factors that impinge on those life-support systems must be observed and respected above human borders and jurisdictions. We must learn to subordinate our needs and priorities to the greater needs of air, water, soil, and biodiversity. But the most important shift that's needed is in our sense of our place in the natural world. We are not above or outside Nature; we are deeply immersed in and dependent on it for our well-being. Seen that way, our constructs — social, economic, political — must respect and conform to the demands of the natural world. A greater sense of respect for other life forms and humility about the extent of what we do know would signal the beginnings of that needed shift.

THE REAL NORTHWEST ECONOMY

W. Ed Whitelaw

ASK NORTHWESTERNERS TO identify the three most important sectors in the Northwest economy, and most of them will
say timber, agriculture, and tourism. It does not seem to matter
which group of Northwesterners you ask. Last year, I asked this
ranking of an audience of graduate students and faculty at a university here in the Northwest, and to a person, they identified timber, agriculture, and tourism as the top three, in that order. I got
the same response from a chamber of commerce audience. And politicians, newspaper editors, and the heads of state and local agencies agree. It is remarkable that such an idea can be so widely held
and so wrong.

139

If we measure economic importance in the Northwest by total
employment in Washington and Oregon, none of these industries
actually ranks in the top three or even the top six. In fact, the top
five are health services and hospitals (about 8 percent of total employment), educational services, schools and colleges (also about 8
percent), business and professional services (about 7 percent),
wholesale trade (about 6 percent), and finance, insurance and real
estate (about 5 percent). Agriculture leads timber and tourism, but

each of the three sectors employs only 2 to 4 percent of the total.

Of the three mythical top sectors, timber always seems to receive the most acclaim. In his December 1991 testimony before the Endangered Species Committee — the so-called God Squad — Con Schallau, the chief economist for the American Forest Resource Alliance, said of Oregon, "Although the relative importance of the forest products industry has declined since 1980, it is still the dominant component." Put some real numbers on this claim, and it vanishes. The number of workers in Oregon's lumber-and-wood-products industry *declined* by 17 percent (13,500 jobs) between 1979 (the year preceding the national recession of the early 1980s) and 1989 (the year preceding the current national recessionary period and long before the spotted owl recovery plan had any impact). By contrast, total employment in Oregon *increased* by 23 percent (257,000 jobs) during the 1979–89 period. Since 1989, timber jobs have continued to decrease while Oregon's total jobs have continued to increase. The timber industry could not be the dominant component of Oregon's economy if, as it contracts, Oregon's economy expands.

Combining Oregon and Washington makes the point even more strongly. Oregon and Washington's lumber-and-wood-products employment *declined* by 20 percent (27,227 jobs) during 1979–89, while total employment in the two states *increased* by 26 percent (751,000 jobs).

Maybe the problem is that those who feel compelled to rank-order industries are not simply counting jobs but have employed some more sophisticated and useful measure. If by "most important" or "dominant" they mean greatest growth in jobs, growth in pay per worker, growth in total payroll, or expected — forecasted — growth in any of these measures, their ranking is still wrong. In fact, by these measures timber and agriculture rank consistently near the bottom. In sharp contrast, most of the sectors that have had the greatest growth in jobs in the recent past also pay more than either timber or agriculture pays. For example, the high-skill, high-pay business and professional services (including advertising agencies, software services, engineering and architectural services, and management consulting) have added more jobs than timber has lost, and these services pay substantially more than timber pays.

Within manufacturing, while the lumber-and-wood-products sector lost 9,996 jobs between 1986–91, a period of expansion common to both Washington and Oregon, the other manufacturing sectors added 70,716 jobs. Not incidentally, these other sectors pay more than the lumber-and-wood-products sector pays. The future promises more of the same. Three of these other manufacturing sectors offer an illustrative contrast with the timber industry in the future. They are electrical machinery, nonelectrical machinery, and instruments. In addition to containing the industries we usually think of as technologically advanced (e.g., computers, semiconductors, and instruments to measure electricity), they include such industries as power hand tools, pumps, refrigeration equipment, light fixtures, household appliances, and dental supplies.

In 1989, these three sectors — electrical machinery, nonelectrical machinery, and instruments, with 91,523 employees, were smaller than the lumber-and-wood-products sector, which employed 107,966 workers. The Fall 1992 *Economic and Revenue Forecast* from both Oregon and Washington disclose that a historic shift in the rank-order of these sectors is taking place. For example, these forecasts predict that by this year employment in lumber and wood products will have fallen to 89,700, while employment in the mostly high-tech sectors will have risen to 90,430. More important, in 1991, the latest year for which I could obtain the data, payroll per worker in lumber and wood products was slightly more than $26,000 while payroll per worker in the three sectors was slightly more than $32, 000, and the latter has been increasing twice as fast as the former.

141

Finally, the sectors that serve tourism, such as lodging and eating places, rank high — though not at the top — in past and expected growth in *jobs*. But they rank quite low in such measures as pay per worker.

No matter how it is managed, the ranking we all believe in has no basis in hard economic fact.

IT IS A bit of a mystery to me why anyone in any region would feel compelled to rank-order industries under any conditions, to find a mythical top three or top dog. I think part of the answer lies with attempting to apply a largely outmoded model of how regional economies grow. This model, which received much attention from regional economists during the immediate post-World War II period, assumed that to grow and prosper, a community, a state, or a region had to attract new dollars from the outside. In its simplistic form, which unfortunately most state and local economic-development specialists adopted enthusiastically, the model implied that if a state or local economy failed to expand its exports, it could not grow and prosper.

So policy makers became obsessed with identifying the principal exporters and elaborating policies favoring the top dogs whose barking apparently would arouse the rest of the economy. On lamentably many occasions over the years, I have heard or read about the so-called opinion leaders — politicians, agency heads, editorial writers, and, especially disappointing, educators — announcing the currently perceived leading industry. Most of the time it has been timber. A former state economic-development official, who no doubt would prefer that I remember him for other statements, was fond of referring to timber as the "mother industry" in the Northwest, apparently choosing to ignore that she was trashing her home and abandoning her children.

These economic-development cheerleaders often concluded that only exports mattered, and specifically, only manufactured exports mattered — that attracting or stimulating manufacturing jobs was a necessary and sufficient precursor for growth in other sectors. But as long ago as 1956, economist Charles Tiebout pointed out in the *Journal of Political Economy* that using this logic means that the only way the world economy could grow and prosper is by exporting to celestial economies. Clearly this is absurd, and a number of other economists now discount the export-base model both because it suffers fatal theoretical flaws and because it yields meaningless, even silly, results.

And the emphasis on manufacturing alone is also wrong. Martin Bailey, an economist at the University of Maryland, stated in a recent newspaper interview, "Competitiveness is not just machinery and semiconductors but the entire economy. The service sector is terribly important to overall living standards." In other words, neither manufacturing nor services is sufficient for a viable economy; both are necessary.

N
W —◇— E
S

IF WE ABANDON the cherished model of the past, can we replace it with something of value, a different, better model, not one demonstrably wrong in its assumptions, facts, and policies? Yes, we can. The Northwest's recent strong growth reflects a multitude of forces and comparative advantages that have been operating in concert for several decades — not the result of the lucky draw of a couple of fast-growing industries. Part of this healthy performance is the evolution of a structure that permits an orderly change: some sectors of the economy mature and decline, while others grow. Twenty-five years ago in *Issues in Urban Economics*, the urban and regional economist Wilbur Thompson anticipated part of what explains Oregon's economic performance:

> *...ALL PRODUCTS WAX and wane, and so the long-range viability of any area must rest ultimately on its capacity to invent and/or innovate or otherwise acquire new export bases. The economic base of the larger metropolitan area is, then, the creativity of its universities and research parks, the sophistication of its engineering firms and financial institutions, the persuasiveness of its public relations and advertising agencies, the flexibility of its transportation networks and utility systems, and all the other dimensions of infrastructure that facilitate the quick and orderly transfer from old dying bases to new growing ones.*

143

These economic attributes that Thompson extols — innovation, creativity, sophistication, persuasiveness, and flexibility — all reflect the well-educated, well-trained technical, administrative, and professional personnel driving the Northwest's economy. Other symptoms illustrate the broad strength of the Northwest's economy. The Portland metropolitan economy, for example, accounting for over half of Oregon's economy and a much greater share of its growth, is among the three or four most diversified metropolitan economies in the country. It is an excellent example of a non-rank-ordered economy, i.e., an economy that is healthy precisely because it does not have a top dog.

To give this structure life, to make it work, one must add a driver, an underlying dynamic mechanism. There is widespread agreement among urban and regional economists in the Pacific Northwest about the extent to which the region's economic growth depends on its reputation for providing residents with a high quality of life. Consider, for example, this statement from John Mitchell, senior vice president and chief economist, U.S. Bancorp, and Paul Sommers, research director, Northwest Policy Center, University of Washington: "Residents and businesses continue to move into the Northwest as more parts of the region are discovered by national and foreign tourists and businesses seeking…favorable living conditions for employees. If [the Northwest] can manage to preserve [its] unique environmental assets…the Northwest will remain one of the strongest regional economies in the country."

Not incidentally, Mitchell and Sommers correctly identify here the salient economic impact of tourism, which is not through the dollars it brings in or the workers it employs but through the number of talented people it persuades to immigrate and stay in the Northwest. Bill Conerly, senior vice president and chief economist for First Interstate Bank of Oregon, characterized the dynamic mechanism succinctly: "People are moving here not because of jobs but because of quality of life.…If people want to live here, jobs will follow."

144 PEOPLE WHO LIVE in the Northwest, therefore, have a choice to make. We must choose between two economic futures. One of these futures — and the policies that get us there — is based on a myth that doesn't serve as explanatory framework for understanding the Northwest's economic future. It generates a flawed model. The other reflects the economic realities of a changing and expanding marketplace.

A few years ago, I had the opportunity to work with several hundred Oregonians, representing business (including the timber industry), labor, academia, and local communities. We wanted to look at alternative ways of solving the state's problems and meeting its challenges. A key to this approach was to reject traditional practices, such as trying to boost the state's timber industry, in favor of alternatives we deemed better able to yield widespread improvement in the standard of living of Oregonians. The document summarizing the plan is called *Oregon Shines: An Economic Strategy for the Pacific Century* (May 1989). The heart of the strategy is summarized in its "Key Strategic Initiatives."

(1) Invest in workers: Oregon can raise the income of its citizens only if communities, businesses, and families increase the education and skills of workers.

(2) Enhance the quality of life: Oregon's quality of life attracts people and advanced industrial firms. Degradation of Oregon's environmental qualities will jeopardize its most important comparative advantage.

Since the publication of this strategic plan, the Oregon Progress Board, chaired by the governor and advised by the Legislature and hundreds of other organizations and individuals, developed a set of measures — called and published as *Oregon Benchmarks* (January 1991) and since then updated — for monitoring and evaluating progress in raising standards of living. The state of Washington and the city of Seattle (and numerous other states and cities across the United States) are exploring this novel approach, complete with monitoring, evaluation, and accountability.

All this, of course, sounds upbeat. It reflects the optimistic assumption that we can perceive the reality of our condition and improve it. But as long as we hold onto the old, comfortable economic myths of our past rather than face the realities of today and tomorrow, the assumption is overly optimistic.

145

In his 1956 book, *The Image: Knowledge in Life and Society*, Kenneth Boulding addresses this point:

What I have been talking about is knowledge. Knowledge, perhaps, is not a good word for this. Perhaps one would rather say my image of the world. Knowledge has an implication of validity, of truth. What I am talking about is what I believe to be true; my subjective knowledge. It is this Image that largely governs my behavior. [The emphasis is Boulding's.]

The behaviors of the press, the politicians, the policy makers, and indeed all of us here in Northwest toward our economy thus are affected by our images of the world. We live in our images. We act on our images. As long as they fail to reflect reality, our economic policies and to a disquieting extent our standards of living will reflect the obsolete memories of our economic past. Such nostalgia will simply impoverish us.

ACKNOWLEDGMENT: William Strange and Ernie Niemi provided editorial assistance and David Helton and Philip Levinson research assistance for this article.

NOTHING NORTH OF DISNEYLAND

Mark Anthony Jarman

Else, if thou refuse to let my people go, behold, tomorrow will I bring the locusts into thy coast: And they shall eat every tree which groweth for you out of the field: And they shall fill thy houses....

Prov. 10

I AM CRUISING America again on I-5's curving ramps and diamond lanes, past my moldy Seattle haunts: the Comet Tavern beside the boxing gym, the Central Tavern in Pioneer Square, Ballard's Owl Cafe, the Squid Row Tavern; we pass through the iron bridges of aubergine Portland, where I buy old Volvo parts and catch Paul DeLay's blues band. He is a wizard on chromatic harmonica. The GMs were horse trading, and I awoke one summer day an indentured servant of the L.A. Kings, the league's famous burial grounds lined with palms. Training camp this year is in a rink in San Diego.

Travel is a pleasant limbo, dazed with distance and wind whistling the vents, inside a particle accelerator with sun and halogen

headlights. It's a long drive down the whole West Coast, considering I won't make the team; they just want me at the camp as an extra body, to knock heads, to scare a few of their lazier D-men. With any luck someone will get injured and they'll have to keep me around. The Intended and I swim in a blue motel pool below a blue motel sky, a daylight moon held in dreamy arms of dead trees. Elderly women in Carmen Miranda bathing caps drag sun cots noisily, fruit shaking on their leather skulls.

My ear is to the Pacific now; I am happy. I like the black of new road, smart yellow stripes leaping, leading me to good diners in Oregon, to a café over a rocky cove and horseshoe beach, mist and sun playing together magically over the free surf. Sometimes it's hard to return to, say, Moose Jaw and the worst winter in twenty years. Down in the States they don't know we live, nothing north of Disneyland really exists. In a deco motel, she gets up while I sleep, gets water and aspirin, decodes the dawn.

WE HIT HAIL in San Francisco, follow I-5 across the spastic L.A. basin's nightmarish beauty of toxins and ice plant and weeping pear, and onto the San Diego freeway, America grinding to a halt in a greasy nitrous mix, a sulfurous fuming, suddenly older than terra cotta, than boxcars. All down I-5, in every city, America grinds its teeth behind the wheel of a bone-weary Hupmobile, becomes little more than a stalled European, pretending it's the new world.

Everywhere in California I see that identical red Spanish tile, stiff dagger plants and indolent palms in the Santa Ana wind. Boy Howdy, she says, someone made a bundle on that Spanish tile. I-5 gets insane; we have to pull off in a beach town and have a breather, a drink, a BLT. Cars slur past full of Guatemalan and Samoan faces, everyone's smashing into each other, not bothering to look at the damage, stay in your car, stop and go, watch for guns, cardiac city. That California is mellow is a myth: it's nuts. But I like its mountain tribes, its third world baroque Babel.

A man is up the palm tree with a chain saw; I didn't know you had to prune those mothers. The California sun we see is eight minutes old. In L.A. the gas station nozzles are like space guns, I

148

couldn't figure out how to use them and felt like an idiot from out of town. I hate being a hick.

HICK OR NOT, I've arrived, and I'm soon pissed as the newt in the local VFW, in the fused Vertebrae of Foreign Wars, in the Stircrazed Lounge & BarBQ, in the Swamp Train, whatever it's called today, where a lone dobro plays sweetly with country and western death, Cajun death, Mississippi death, the mystery train. A bartender called Ohio opens and closes the refrigerator in this favored, favored nightspot. "I'm your biggest fan." Who said that? I think I imagined it. On the jukebox, on the stage, country and western death relocates to the suburbs, opens and closes. America conquers and is conquered in the same spin cycle. After the drive-by shooting, Channel 7 asks everyone, How does it feel? On the jukebox Bob Dylan asks, How does it feel? A waitress moves languidly in the long aisle to your distant table. In L.A., when a King is dead there is another King. As the newest player, I'm interviewed on the cable channel no one watches. The interviewer brings up thirteen-year-old hookers. Perhaps this is his interest. It seems off-topic. I went to the radio interview, ended up alone at the microphone.

WITH THREE DAYS to kill, we cross the border at San Ysidro, cross green streaks of traffic into the Baja Peninsula. A man breathes fire on the street of a small market town, asks me for change. Pesos, sure, *de nada*. The dollar is killing the peso. Down by the fishing docks gray sharks hang in gray sky's rain, rain a gray noise, sharks slick. Their skin is harsh but also a little like the feel of a cold puck. The Intended's camera clicks, blood on wood, some tails still hanging on rope after the shark is cut down and gone. Those strange shark eyes, the size of a camera lens, still seeming to see us and say, *Just give me a minute alone with one of you motherfuckers that nailed me.* I want to freeze one and take it home, over those bloodless lines on the map. Pretend I pulled it out of my lake in Canada.

149

MEXICAN INFLATION TO TOP 100%

The bordellos got shut down while we were in one city and hundreds of hoolicij started peeling in front of the Government Palace to protest. All these Mexican women pulling their dresses up and sideways; it was out of Fellini.

BUSINESS COUNCIL REPORT SAYS MEXICO WILL SUFFER

At the border a billboard on a hill. The Intended provides me with a rough translation: "That which you earn in Mexico, spend in Mexico." The road climbs toward the fences. The illegals stream into El Norte, waiting all day, back and forth, get busted and start over, running like ghosts through the cars at the crossing; the guards give up and the river grinds its teeth at night. The American Customs has glass doors like a supermarket. There are stainless steel tables. No one stops me at the border: I have a green card, a Canadian passport. They would kill for what I take for granted. How many souls are here waiting in this limbo? Millions: No one can supply exact numbers. Gavilondo and a hundred other chaotic neighborhoods tilt on the plateau; here are our lost jobs, the *maquiladoras*, the assembly plants, a big toxic fingerprint pressed under the border, a web of river canyons and sewage, a bruise spreading below the skin. Established families live at the dump, like seagulls picking through the trash mountains. At least seagulls can fly to the sea at nightfall. Newcomers, perhaps Guatemalans, set up shacks or crates in the riverbed, gambling it won't rain. Eventually it will rain.

150

THE ANTHEMS

I go to camp and I agree to go primitive. The powers that be like to see us peons duke it out, a feeding frenzy, a big rage.

There are two training camps: one for rookies, minor league migrants, free agents, walk-on dark horses, goons with hearts of gold, etc. The second camp is for the big club. They say I'm overweight, which I always am, and put me in the early camp. They don't want me. The sleek shall inherit the earth. I start one scrap with comedy: "Feel lucky, punk?" My hand gets cut to rat shit on his helmet. You hit your thirties and bopping someone in the dentures doesn't have the same cachet as when you're a sparkplug teen scrambling to make a team for the first time. Now I feel sheepish, a carnival geek of sorts. This profession lacks dignity, punching plastic headgear when all I want is a piece of the peace that passeth all understanding. Feel stupid, punk? You will.

The young players dress so well now, like *GQ* models: loafers with no socks, sharp hair, stockbroker trench coats, and muscle tone a-go-go. They drive new four-by-fours and Firebirds. After the game I go for a beer. "No thanks," they say, "got to work out, pump iron. Maybe later." Maybe later they'll start resembling us, scarred and driving pickups, or beaters, smashing glasses in some crappy lounge, daring the bouncers to toss us out. I was always on the wrong end of a three-way contract: X amount with Regina Pats (later shipped to Kamloops), XX amount with Flint, Michigan, in the "I", XXX amount if I cracked the Minnesota lineup. Someone doesn't like your face, sends you down, and just like that you lose $100,000. I had chances at scholarships, but school didn't seem there back then. Who went to school? For what?

One player borrows money off absolutely everyone, including the Zamboni driver and the Down's syndrome kid hanging around the team, then the player leaves town. He knew he was cut.

After the brawl the ref calls the game; we walk to our dressing room yelling what a bunch of fucking cunts they are for starting it, while they walk to the visitors room (where we keep the heat on high to drain them) yelling what a bunch of fucking cunts we are for starting it, all of us sincerely believing we're the good guys, the wronged party. Let the galled jade wince, our withers are unwrung.

How many times have I heard the anthems?

Speed up. Stop. Skate forward, circle back. Hurry up and stop. Go! Seal off their blue line, pinch in, stand up to them at our blue line.

Choppers buzz the beach, flapping the palms. There is blue light in insect wings, my skin actually becoming more humid, soft versus Alberta.

"Come on, up the boards, up the boards. No, not that way. I SAID UP THE GODDAM BOARDS!"

"PAY THE PRICE!" yells the coach, and as a joke we imitate him. Any stupid play and we jump up. "Pay the price! Pay the price!" He doesn't get it.

WE DO A fast road trip, and all immediately catch the Hong Kong flu. I'm in the penalty box, and our team scores twice shorthanded; what lesson do we take from this? Also, why do I play better when I'm sick as a dog? The whole team is palsied and coughing, but we win. The Vancouver sports writer was pissed off at my suspension in Detroit. This'll make the peaceniks happy, he says. A good fight never hurt anyone, he says.

Yeah, sure, as long as he's not in it.

I KEEP BREAKING my fingers over and over on helmets. My hands are wrecked. I soak them in warm wax after a fight, have to keep punching plastic hoping one will connect, maybe break a nose. I use wax, ice packs, tape, butterfly stitches, vitamin E, whirlpools, massage, you name it. Outside, spring rain falls under the traffic lights and colored wires, the crowd wet and smiling after the game, faces like open leaves, and me inside the huge arena with my hands smashed to shit because I had to fight again with bad hands and make them worse and worse. I'll be sixty-five and my hands will kill me. I know it. I'm not big, maybe 190. I earn my money. I get in my tiny car, hunched and small in a big country, and I put my hands on the wheel feeling meanness and a new kind of crappy. I'm being used, but I continue in that knowledge, at times buying into it. I put my hands on the wheel.

The gold and gray sky at our heads, a million birds under a streaked golden bowl. A low, swift chopper falls from the gyrating palms, falls into La Jolla's sweet erosion of surf, bounces like a Christmas bauble, flailing and whooshing and cutting the heads off the waves. In sunglasses, we line the shore. They clamber from the bubble dazed, and we cheer like a puzzling Pepsi ad.

I FEEL LIKE Chicken Little; everywhere I go things fall from the sky. I favor drab clothes, shades, the solemn nod of the good bartender. "I thank you," he says politely.

Bozos in the stand yell for Baumgartner, wanting the other coach to tap him on the shoulder, send him out scrap. "DROP THE BAUM! DROP THE BAUM!!" It's me they want the bomb dropped on, huge hands clapping as if in slow motion.

The handsome player from Atlanta wanted to take us out for dinner. His fiancée, my fiancée. He asked the waiter to give him the tab.

Later I took the waiter aside. "He pays for too many, give it to me." He gave me the bill. The handsome player from Atlanta lifted the waiter by his lapels. The waiter's feet dangling. "If I say give me the bill, I MEAN GIVE ME THE FUCKING BILL! Understand, Jack?" A pleasant interlude.

WE DRIVE UNDER electric palm trees etched in yellow and green, striking, hallucinatory. A woman's gauzy skirt holds to her legs, shows her as if there is no material. Perfect coiffures crash into pools, waiting for Prince Charming, waiting for the oysters to kick in. We pull in Mexican radio.

The coach pulls all three goalies; this must be a record. I get a penalty, and the organ player does "Darling, You... Send Me."

In the last minute their winger kicks in a goal, and they claim a shot from the point hit me and went in. The referee says it's in. I can't believe it. "This isn't World Cup soccer," I say to the ref, "the guy kicked it in!" Later in the bar their winger admits to me that he booted the puck in, but it's too late for us to change anything. The visiting team is thrown out of the first hotel, the visiting team is thrown out of the second hotel. They still win.

The coach stops the bus at a freeway phone, tells us he's calling the farm team and bringing up five players. We sit and watch him gyrate on the phone outside. Next game we're a little sharper.

The reporter says, "Drinkwater, it's been an up and down year." I tell him I prefer to think of it as sideways, backwards, crablike. My shirt is strobing on the TV monitor.

THE TV'S EVENING news is depressingly similar in L.A., Chicago, Miami, San Diego, etc. Traffic seizes, guns out, an exponential equation. I want to live in the desert, listen to Gram Parsons, drive empty spaces. Others can have the coasts. I feel the pull but don't want to be another lemming.

Oranges shake, their orchard a hod of coals. (Whoever is not written in the book will be cast into the lake of fire, and whoever is not written in the book will find his ass down on the farm team, choking chickens.) The Mexican and Central American field hands live on *nada*, their heads turn to watch me walk past. They stand in somber groups on Encinitas Boulevard, waiting for work, for the jobs we won't do. They move around with their hometown half-gods, like us welcoming what kills them. They live illegally on the hill above the mall. February brings frost down on the orchards, rueful red-eyed hawks. When winter rains run off the Spanish tiles I think of children living in the dump, parasites moving toward their small bare feet; when it rains I think of those in the riverbed. Are they drowning even now as I lie in bed? Are they stealing across yet another frontier, visiting the undiscovered country? My Intended watches another dawn walk over the border, and I dream a shot coming right at my face, can hear the awful sound as the puck flattens my eye. I jump up in bed. I think of the shark's eye. What's wrong? she asks. Bob Dylan and Channel 7 ask, How does it feel? Well, it's difficult to distill. We're on the edge, we're on the edge of a huge desert that blooms just once a year, you can blink or sleep through it.

MATT WUERKER

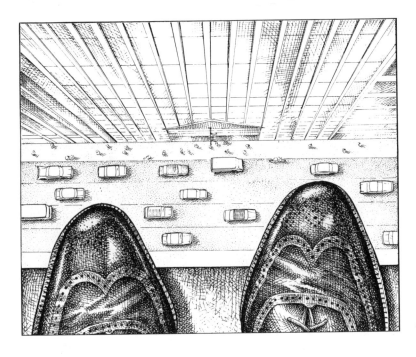

ON NOT
SPEAKING
FRENCH

Robert Sheckley

I LIVED IN Paris for a number of years without speaking any but the most rudimentary French. This was not mere laziness, nor was it linguistic pathology; there was an ideological basis to my refusal to learn the language of Pétain and Molière. It went a lot farther than "didn't get around to it," though that played its part, too.

Basically, I didn't want to learn French for what I thought were good and sufficient reasons, and, despite social pressures, remained true to my ideal.

Why did I take this position? First of all, as a working writer, my only tool and resource is the English/American language. It is this language that gives me my tongue, that informs my dreams. In this tongue are the dead bodies of my masters, Shakespeare and Milton, Thackerey and Dickens, Graham Greene and Eric Ambler, and of the American writers, Melville and Poe, and so many others. For me to approach France without the lift and swell of my own language to support me would have left me mute indeed.

Paris was a place of the heart for me many years before I ever got there, and remains so today. My Paris was created for me long before I got there by Dumas, Victor Hugo, Maupassant, Baudelaire,

and many others. For me they all wrote in English, for that was the language in which I read them. The pictures they painted in my mind came to me exclusively in the English language. And so Paris became an English place, but a foreign one, like Key West or New Orleans or Valpariso or Peking, all of which also came to me via English.

Paris was more than the other cities, though. Paris was a capital of one of the great realms of the unknown. It was the place of French genius, a genius so astounding that it was an amazing privilege just to walk the streets of the city of light. I didn't even have to be happy there. To suffer in Paris was, for a while at least, better than to live happily in America. "Better fifty years of Europe than a cycle of Cathay!" The words are by Tennyson, but Montaigne, another of my heroes, could happily have quoted them.

My life in Paris was splendid and terrible and had nothing to do with painfully trying to eke out a sentence in some language I didn't speak and didn't want to speak, except perfectly. But even perfect French would have been a problem for me as an American writer. And I had some experience in this regard. I had already noted how Spanish, with which I had some slight facility, had infected the language in my head in which I talk to myself. A foreign language is like an infection of the word-creating facility. My knowledge of Spanish put Spanish words into my interior world, and these sometimes came out as I wrote in my English. I was sick of striking *Aye, Caramba!* out of my sentences, sick of thinking *lo siento mucho* when I meant I was sorry. What was I to do with these foreign borrowings that were now lodged in my head? I did not want them as part of my writing vocabulary but there they were anyhow. Those Spanish words and phrases — *no hay de que* — think nothing of it — were as much a part of my day-to-day vocabulary as my English words. And some of those words were very fine indeed. I thrill still to *La valle de los caidos*, and to Calderon's line, *Que desconsada la vida!* Lorca still lurks within me, almost blotted out by the Guardia Civil in Granada.

But delicious though I found some of these images, wrapped in the mystery of their foreign sounds, I knew that they had no part

in my work and my life, which was to write in the English language as I understood it.

The Spanish infection was manageable because I didn't have too much of it. And frankly, Spanish, for me, is not a very seductive tongue, or should I say infectious? French is a different proposition. I speak here, not from any book-knowledge of what a language is like on the inside, but from my own feelings about it.

To speak French badly was unthinkable. To speak it well was dangerous. To speak it at all would be to give up one of the main reasons I had come to Paris — to walk the streets and not understand a word of what was going on around me. What bliss!

Perhaps you need to be a natural solitary to like that sort of thing. I liked it very much. Parisian sounds were enchanting, and the language was music to the ears, as long as I didn't have to understand what the people were talking about. It was a continuing pleasure for me to walk the streets and listen to the everyday music of conversation. And to watch the faces! They are so much more vivid when you don't know what they're saying. And all of this was superimposed over images of the literary Paris I had been absorbing for so many years. Victor Hugo's Paris of dandies like Marius, stern older man like Jean Valjean, women like Cosette. The Paris opera evoked The Phantom of the Opera. A street named Gitle-chat was music and enchantment, and I am fortunate to not know still what it means. Please don't write in and tell me!

And there were intimate pleasures, too. I walked through the Paris of the American writer Robert W. Chambers, whose negligible fantasies of artist's life in turn of the century Paris filled my soul when I was a child planning my eventual escape from Maplewood, New Jersey, a town in a country where I understood everyone very well and yearned to be among strangers whom I couldn't understand at all. Perhaps back then I did understand something about understanding. It seemed to me that I could understand people and things better if I couldn't interpret the sound-balloons above their heads that they spoke in. If I heard their words only as music.

As far as practical difficulties went, there were few. I knew a number of people in Paris at that time, both French and foreign. The

French never expected me to learn French. Listening to their tortured and rudimentary English, I could understand why. For the French, language is something that expresses the soul, and you don't exchange your soul for another. If you have an American soul, so be it, leave well enough alone.

After the success of my experiment in not learning French, I tried it again with Greek. I had a very good time in Greece and the islands. I attribute it to not speaking Greek. What was there to say? Was I to talk to people about the price of fish, or whatever disastrous thing had happened recently in local politics? The Greeks did not expect me to know Greek, and would have considered it an aberration if I had tried. But then, most of the Greeks I knew were language-intoxicated, in love with their old gods and their old books. They communicated that to me very well. If I wanted to hold a proper conversation, there was always an English speaker not too far away.

And this was certainly true in Paris, where everyone speaks some English whether they admit it or not. It is, after all, every American's second home. The English come there in droves. English has such a vogue as everyone's second language that there's never any problem striking up a conversation.

As to practicalities, again, I had no trouble at all. Learning the Metro system in Paris is simple. Learning the bus routes is not much more difficult. It's always best to find your own way around a city without asking questions. Why on earth should you have to bother some native with your questions about how to get to the Sacre Coeur, for example, when half the resources of France are at your disposal to get you to whatever touristic place you want to get to? The French recognize that the great tourist spots — Sacre Coeur, Montmartre, Montparnasse, the Boulevard Saint-Germain, Notre Dame, San Michel, and so on, are the common property of the world, and not exclusively for the French.

Ordering in a restaurant is no trouble at all. An interest in French food requires little French. And waiters always seem able to communicate with you if you don't know if a particular item is fish or fowl or good red meat.

You can eat and you can get around Paris without French. You can fall in love without French. In fact, you can fall in love better without French than with it. A look and a sigh does more to further love than all the explanations in the world. And, too, the French are not high-flown talkers about these matters of love, despite their reputation. Rather cynical, if you ask me. I'd rather love the French than listen to them.

Movies are subtitled. The ones that are available only in French can usually be safely avoided.

For checking into a hotel, they'll read your mind. No language of any sort is necessary. Sign language suffices to ask, Do you have so and so many francs? Good. Here is your room, there is your bed, and there's a complimentary breakfast of *café au lait* and croissant. Nothing could be simpler.

In fact, your problems in France only come when you decide that you want to learn the language. In order to converse, I suppose, because you don't need it for any other reason. That's when you change archetypes. You leave ancient and beloved Paris of winding streets and mist-draped lamplights, of alchemist towers and low bridges, for the world of precise pronunciations and rules of the subjunctive and making sense of alien word-orders. This is fine if that's what you want. If that's the archetype you're going for, more power to you. But I was able to think of better ways of spending my time than in a Berlitz school, and better uses for my thoughts than the contemplation of passive voices.

But on this matter of love, it is quite fine to fall in love with a person with whom you don't share a word in common. In a little known variant of the ancient Greek myth, Ariadne and Theseus were great together as long as they had no language in common. Theseus spoke the broad Doric of the peninsula, whereas Ariadne's language was Cretan infected with North African borrowings. They made a great couple. But on the boat that they took back to Athens, Ariadne began to learn Greek. She showed great proficiency. Within a day or two, she had enough of a basic vocabulary to say to Theseus, "We need to talk about our relationship." Hearing this, Theseus made for the island of Naxos. Here he put Ariadne ashore, and said he'd be back later. And then he sailed for Athens. Ariadne was stuck, until she later met Dionysus, who was always ready to

161

talk about relationships. He was that kind of guy.

Ever since, men have known that the language of love is silence, and Paris is the city of love because for a non-French speaker it is silent and deficient in explanations. Sometimes in Paris there is a moment when you don't understand what's going on, and therein lies its charm.

THE AUTHORS

Diana Abu-Jaber's excerpt is from her forthcoming novel *Memories of Birth*. "The gist of the story comes from my grandmother who was an amazing role model. She married my grandfather at age fourteen and had seventeen children. When she moved into the desert with my grandfather, who was a descendent of Bedouins, she built one of the first libraries in Jordan in her home because so many people brought books to her." Diana's first novel was *Arabian Jazz*, and she has short fiction forthcoming in *Story* and *Kenyon Review*. She teaches creative writing at the University of Oregon as well as Third World and Middle Eastern culture and literature.

James Aho is Professor of Sociology at Idaho State University in Pocatello where he teaches social theory, symbolic sociology, and religion. His latest book, forthcoming in 1994, is *This Thing of Darkness: A Sociology of the Enemy*. "The 'Ken' referred to in the epigram is my own son. I think it illustrates the fluidity of ethnic borders in our times."

Larry Colton is currently living in the border town of Hardin, Montana, researching a book on the Crow Indians, focusing on their championship girls basketball team. "The high point of my year here was being adopted into the Crow tribe." He wrote two books; the last one, *Goat Brothers*, was a 1993 main selection for the Book of the Month Club. Larry has also written for the *N.Y. Times Magazine*, *Esquire*, *Sports Illustrated*, *Philadelphia Inquirer*, the *Oregonian*, and *Ladies Home Journal*.

Michael Dorris, an anthropologist and author, visited refugee camps in Zimbabwe during 1991 in his capacity as a board member of Save the Children Foundation. *Rooms in the House of Stone* was the result of a series of essays from that trip. He has written a short story collection, *Working Men*; *The Broken Cord*; *A Yellow Raft in Blue Water*; and a children's book, *Morning Girl*. Michael also wrote *The Crown of Columbus* with his wife, Louise Erdrich.

Virginia Flynn is an artist who lives a colorful life in Portland, Oregon creating black and white illustrations of people and places she's never seen before.

Hollis Giammatteo was born and raised on the East Coast. "Recently I've traded one set of boundaries for another — a city's for an island's. I moved from Seattle, where I lived for twelve years, to Lopez Island, a place defined by the boundary of its shores, and where peoples' choices reflect the limitations imposed by our geography. A good example? The ferries. Our limitations reflect, by the same token, the boundaries of separate skins, in spite of what the 'new' physics and Buddhism counsel. I've been a writer for two decades now, having splashed around in myriad forms — poetry, plays, fiction, and magazine nonfiction, and been published in *Ms*, *Vogue*, *Prairie Schooner*, and *Calyx*. This piece for *Left Bank* is in some way my attempt to understand, by the process of writing, the boundaries I impose, looking out through my filters of class, race, and gender. I write to heal those gaps and only hope that my words have an impact on my behavior."

Robert Heilman is a writer and storyteller who lives near Myrtle Creek, in the Oregon zone of Occupied Jefferson. The border he knows best is the poverty line, near which he's lived for over twenty-three years. His work has appeared in dozens of periodicals including *Harper's Magazine*, *The Oregonian*, *Seattle Weekly* and *The Congressional Record*. "If at First You Don't Secede...." is from *Manual Labor (and other things not taught in schools)* a "highly acclaimed, timely, and insightful, yet (regrettably) unpublished collection of essays."

Andy Helman is a writer who continually crosses the borders of print journalism and broadcasting, but doesn't reveal the fact often because of the nearsighted, one-column boundaries the revelation often creates. Her articles have appeared in the national slicks and she has written for corporate, cable, public, and commercial broadcasting. She is Executive Producer for *Upon Reflection*, which airs on KCTS-TV, Seattle.

Christopher Howell, who was born in Portland and taught in NW colleges, is currently director of Creative Writing at Emporia State University in Kansas. "For me the writing of the poem had to do with television, how it brings into our homes images of such astonishing brutality and suffering and how we have learned, somehow, to respond blandly, as though these outrages were part of the programming — and, ironically I suppose, that is exactly what they are to the technicians, producers, and so-called news people who arrange them for us. One sixth of the world is either starving or dog-paddling right at the starvation line; wars erupt everywhere like blown gaskets. When will we actually know the situation of beings on this planet? Or, in keeping with your theme, when will we cross the border, tear the veil, between sight and understanding?"

Mark Anthony Jarman, a graduate of the Iowa Writers Workshop, lives in Victoria, B.C. He is the author of *Dancing Nightly in the Tavern*, a collection of stories; *Killing the Swan*, poetry; and editor of an anthology, *Ounce of Cure*, published by Beach Holme.

Christi Killien co-authored with Sheila Bender *Writing in a Convertible with the Top Down: A Unique Guide for Writers*. She is also the author of six fiction books for children and young adults. "The Curse" is part of a collection of essays entitled *Breast in the Bone*. "It is a memoir of sorts, although I'm writing thematically about both my family's past and the present...I thought that 'The Curse' described the boundaries that exist between generations in a family."

Mercedes Lawry is the communications director for a child advocacy organization in Seattle. She has been published in *New Virginia Review*, *Hawaii Pacific Review*, *Caliban*, *Blue Mesa Review*, *Indiana Review*, and also writes fiction and stories for children. She was the recipient of Artist Trust GAP Grant and won first prize in poetry in the 1990 Indiana Poetry & Fiction Contest (*Sycamore Review*).

Christopher Merrill's *Only the Nails Remain: Three Balkan Journeys*, from which "Kosovo" is excerpted, will be published in 1994. His other books are *The Grass of Another Country: A Journey Through the World of Soccer* and *The Forgotten Language: Contemporary Poets and Nature*, both from Henry Holt. "It's the most terrifying thing

to be shelled by these people and then watch NATO planes flying overhead. We're looking at the same set of circumstances as World War II except from the beginning we've known about the genocide. It's almost the same agenda except the Serbs are more brutal, less organized....My god, this is just so awful, how do these people survive it? Yet they do survive it. This summer they were planting gardens....I often thought as I traveled around Yugoslavia that what I saw was not unique. It doesn't take very many steps to go from something that looks innocuous to turn into something lethal....The effort to honor and be realistic about what other people are about, that's what we need to do."

Mary Misel is a shipyard electrician by trade and has been writing poetry since she was fourteen. She has been published in *Stanza, NW Literary Review, Upper Left Edge,* and *Tradeswomen's Network Newsletter.*

Jennifer Mitton's story is from her newly finished collection. "I was recently told that 'The Last Ferry' is a great story, but that women should not feel guilt for having abortions. How harsh we are to expect ourselves to have evolved beyond such feelings of guilt or to suppress the ones that linger. I see no merit in systematically creating female characters whose strength and optimism outstrips my own. More important to my story is the interaction between conflicting parts of each character and between the characters themselves. Their sensitivity to each other is so great that their very boundaries become blurred, and in their resulting distress I see a rounder truth and a more accepting vision of what it means to be alive." Jennifer is a novelist, reviewer, teacher, and short story writer in Vancouver, B.C. Her first novel *Fadimatu,* set in Nigeria and published by Goose Lane Editions, was a 1992 finalist for the F.G. Bressani Prize. Her stories have been selected for anthologies and have appeared in *The Malahat Review, The New Quarterly,* and *Prairie Journal of Canadian Literature.*

Ken Olsen is a newspaper reporter and freelance writer living near Pullman, Washington. He is co-author of *Cross-Country Skiing Yellowstone Country.* His stories have been published by *Outside, Kinesis Magazine,* and *High Country News.*

Henk Pander, born and educated in The Netherlands, has had one-man shows in The United States and The Netherlands. He has designed over twenty stage sets, and his paintings and drawings have been commissioned by many museums and institutions, including the National Aeronautics & Space Administration and the State of Oregon for the State Capitol Building. Henk's art has been published in a wide range of books and magazines, among them *20th Century Masters of Erotic Art* (Crown), *New York Review of Books, Dance Magazine, Arts and Architecture,* and *Parabola Magazine.*

Bob Pyle has written, among other books,*Wintergreen*, recipient of the 1987 John Burroughs Medal, and *The Thunder Tree: Lessons From an Urban Wildland.* He is currently working on a book of personal nonfiction inspired by Bigfoot, the subject of a 1989 Guggenheim Fellowship, and a novel. "I have been thinking a lot about borders while working on *Across the Dark Divide* — watersheds, lightnesses and darknesses, the murky line between ourselves and other sentient beasts. But recent losses among friends and mentors have put me much in mind of the Big Border — the one we all hope to avoid for a long time. The twin insults in this piece came together nicely, reconciling themselves in a comforting image of ultimate afterlife, among the dirt and new growth."

Sandra Scofield, a native Texan and long-time resident of Oregon, has been writing fiction and poetry for over twenty years. She has published four novels. *Beyond Deserving* (a finalist for the National Book Award) and *Walking Dunes* are available in Plume paperback editions. *More Than Allies* was released in November, 1993, and a fifth novel is slated for June, 1994 from Villard. Scofield, who says for most of her life there have been "these days, vast and flat as the Staked Plains," finds writing is the coyote that takes her across the border, from despair to equanimity, on a road marked "Happy," with no distance named.

Robert Sheckley has lost count, but says he's written at least fifty books. Several recent titles are: *Bring Me the Head of Prince Charming* and *If at Faust You Don't Succeed* (both with Roger Zelazny); *The Alternative Detective*; and coming sometime in 1994, *Aretino* (working title of the third book in the series with Roger Zelazny). In addition to being the fiction editor for *Omni Magazine* in the early '80s, Robert has written film and TV scripts, and feature films have been made based on his books.

William Stafford, Oregon's Poet Laureate for many years and one of the widest-read poets in the United States, died at age seventy-nine shortly after he submitted his poem. He was a generous supporter of small presses including *Left Bank*. Recent publications include: *The Animal That Drank Up Sound* (a children's book, illustrated by Debra Frasier), Harcourt, Brace, Jovanovich, 1992; *My Name is William Tell*, Confluence Press, 1992; *Seeking The Way*, (with illuminations by Robert Johnson), Melia Press, Minneapolis, 1992.

David Suzuki, Professor of Zoology at the University of British Columbia, is the host of Canadian Broadcast Company's television show, *The Nature of Things*. He has written fifteen books including science books for children. With Joseph Levine, David wrote *The Secret of Life, Redesigning the Living World*, which is the companion book to the PBS series of the same name.

Kathleen Tyau is currently working on a book of Hawaiian stories to be published in 1994 by Farrar, Straus & Giroux. She recounts a border incident. "When the inspector at the train station in Vancouver, B.C., asked me if I was taking any food back to the United States, I replied, 'Yes, a 500-year-old duck egg.' My aunt had bought the egg for me in Chinatown, and I looked forward to sharing it with my friends in Portland. He asked to see this egg. I produced it, still encased in layers of clay, sawdust, and paper. 'What's inside?' he asked. I described the hard gray shell, the 'white' of the duck egg aged into black gelatin, the gray paste of its yolk. I didn't tell him that one of those eggs fed my whole family when I was a child. I didn't say that I held my breath to block out the ammonia smell and bitter taste but ate my portion without complaint. 'It may not really be 500 years,' I added. 'Maybe more like 50 or 100. They exaggerate.' I waited for him to crack open the shell to see if I was telling the truth. I mean, wouldn't you be curious? Wouldn't you check for diamonds or opium? Instead, he threw 500 years of my cultural heritage, more or less, into the garbage can and waved me onto the train."

W. Ed Whitelaw is President of ECO Northwest, an economic consulting firm in Eugene and Portland, Oregon, and Professor of Economics at the University of Oregon.

Matt Wuerker is a cartoonist who lives in Portland, Oregon.

WESTERN STATES BOOK AWARDS
1   9   9   3

FICTION
The Hedge, The Ribbon
Carol Orlock
BROKEN MOON PRESS
272 Pages, 6" x 9"
ISBN 0-913089-48-6 $13.95 Paper

CREATIVE NONFICTION
Two Old Women
Velma Wallis
EPICENTER PRESS
160 Pages, 5" x 7"
ISBN 0-945397-18-6 $16.95 Cloth

POETRY
August Zero
Jane Miller
COPPER CANYON PRESS
96 Pages, 6" x 9"
ISBN 1-55659-060-1 $22.00 Cloth / -061-X $12.00 Paper

For more information, contact Western States Arts Federation (WESTAF)
236 Montezuma Avenue, Santa Fe, New Mexico 87501

505-988-1166 ■ TDD 505-988-5278 ■ FAX 505-982-9307

LEFT BANK

A new way to read between the lines —
a potlatch of pointed prose and poetry.

Semiannual in December & June, Left Bank is a book series featuring NW writers on universal themes. Readers are treated to a provocative, entertaining, and evocative cross-section of creative nonfiction, fiction, essays, interviews, poetry, and art.

Themes are determined by an editorial staff and advisory board of respected writers, editors, and publishers from Alaska, British Columbia, Idaho, Montana, Oregon, and Washington.

> **#1: *Writing & Fishing the Northwest*** — Consider the cast. Wallace Stegner, Greg Bear, Craig Lesley, Sharon Doubiago, Nancy Lord, John Keeble, and others.

> **#2: *Extinction*** — Get it before it's gone. David Suzuki introduces Tess Gallagher, Barry Lopez, David Quammen, Sallie Tisdale, Robert Michael Pyle, John Callahan, Nancy Lord, and others.

> **#3: *Sex, Family, Tribe*** — get intimate with Ursula Le Guin, Ken Kesey, William Stafford, Colleen McElroy, Matt Groening, William Kittredge, Charles Johnson, and many more.

> **#4: *Gotta Earn a Living*** — the work of two baker's dozen, including Norman Maclean, Kate Braid, Gary Snyder, David Duncan, Teri Zipf, Sherman Alexie, Sibyl James, and Robin Cody.

> **#5: *Border & Boundaries*** — you've got it.

> **#6: *Kid's Stuff*** — Ann Rule, Virginia Euwer Wolff, and Sherman Alexie join twenty others in a look at kids — how we treat 'em and how we don't — how we write about childhood and what we write for children. These and a host of other angles will be explored.

BOOKSTORES, SEE COPYRIGHT PAGE FOR ORDERING INFORMATION. INDIVIDUALS, PHOTOCOPY THE ORDER FORM ON THE LAST PAGE, OR PICK UP *LEFT BANK* AT YOUR FAVORITE BOOKSTORE.

REQUEST OUR CATALOG. AND ASK FOR WRITERS' GUIDELINES — YOU JUST NEVER KNOW.

LEFT BANK

— a great gift to give yourself or any thoughtful friend who enjoys the adventure of superb writing. Just photocopy this page, fill in the form below, and send it today. Subscriptions are $16, postage paid, and begin with the next issue/ edition to be published. Back-numbers 1–4 are available for $7.95; Numbers 5+ are $9.95 each; add $2.50 shipping for the first book and 75¢ for each additional.

Send Left Bank to me at:

Send a gift subscription to:

I'd like the following back issues (see previous page):

My order total is:

I've enclosed a check or Money Order — or charge my VISA or MC; its number and expiration are:

VISA/MC orders (no subs) may now be placed toll-free at 800.858.9055